I Am NOT A Dirty Bitch

by

Lynne P. McDougall

For all of those still existing with the shame associated with historical sexual abuse

To
    Noelle
True freedom is
  Letting go of the
      Past

    Love
      Lynne x
            February
              2022

The book you are about to read is not a perfect literacy masterpiece, it no doubt contains minor errors which have not been detected during editing, I hope this does not distract you from the message of the book.
However, just like the book, I too am not a perfect copy, but this is me and this is my story.

DISCLAIMER

Contents

Foreword

There is no doubt that society is only just beginning to face the thorny issue of child sexual abuse. It has become evident in recent times the depth of the problem we, as a society, must address. The constant news headlines of institutional abuse and the cover-ups of those at the top, who should know better, appear endless.

It is clear that abuse can also take place in the home, sometimes by those closest to the victims, by those who should be protecting the child and making home the safe place it needs to be.

Lynne's groundbreaking book not only covers all aspects of child sexual abuse but also details her own story as a victim. She has spent decades compiling her own research and helping others deal with the emotional roller coaster that life becomes. I have worked for over twenty years as a registered psychotherapist. Clients come to me with a variety of problems ranging from anxiety and depression to chronic fatigue syndrome. When we start looking at cause, I'm sad to say the emotional issues nearly always go back to childhood and in so many cases are attached to sexual abuse.

Lynne has been extremely brave in writing this book. Her will to help others and raise awareness has overridden an inner wish to hide her past. I commend this very special book not only to victims as a self-help guide but to the public at large to raise awareness of what might be happening around you and perhaps give you the courage to speak out and help.

Tony Clarkson – Registered psychologist
Founder of The Sanctuary of Healing

Introduction

I Am NOT A Dirty Bitch is a story of a challenging childhood centred on sexual abuse, physical abuse, emotional abuse and neglect, which are often interwoven into the fabrics of a dysfunctional family.

It is a story of hope and encouragement for victims of historical child sexual abuse, (CSA); a journey of discovery providing the tools and support needed for the reader to embark upon their own journey from victim to survivor. The title I Am NOT A Dirty Bitch is significant; 'dirty bitch' was the response from my mother when I told her about being sexually abused.

By sharing my journey from victim to thriver and what it entailed it is hoped that you may identify with the pain and emotional baggage I carried along with the identified traits that many victims possess. Whilst the events of my childhood will no doubt be very different to your situation, you may identify with my emotional pain that will resurface in you as you identify and connect to me as a kindred spirit.

My hope is that you too can move forward, letting go of any guilt and shame you may carry whilst learning to love and care for yourself.

Whilst there is information available on the internet for the victims of child sexual abuse, I have come across very little in the form of a structured book which sets out a clear proposal for recovery written by someone who has personal experiences of child sexual abuse and does not reside in the USA, where the majority of self-help books originate.

Never before in history has child sexual abuse been so much in the headlines with renowned celebrities being convicted of their crimes and being punished for their actions. No sooner are statistics released than they become outdated as new cases of historic child sexual abuse are highlighted by the media. It has been said that this is only the tip of the iceberg due to its secretive nature. The crime is often contained and restrained deep within the victims and the true picture will never be fully recognised. Due to its recent coverage many victims are now ready to address the past and move on from the shame and the guilt, I use the term COMING OUT.

My COMING OUT took place in September of 2012 when I told my mother that I was NOT a dirty bitch and that she would never call me that again. I reminded her that I was a child of seven when it started. She as my mother should have stopped the abuse and protected me. My words obviously hit a truth; she slammed the phone down. There was no further contact between us for four years.

When I was living with my dark secret each time there was a reference to CSA on the TV I would either go out of the room or change the channel, too many painful memories would come flooding back. At that point I chose to suppress them, in an attempt to avoid the pain. Now they no longer have any control over me I can tell people that I was a victim of CSA without feeling the shame and humiliation. I now no longer see myself as damaged, contaminated goods; these were the labels I placed on myself in accordance with the law of low self-esteem and image. As a child I did believe it really was my fault and that I was a dirty bitch, which over the years was reinforced by my mother's cruel tongue.

It was Dame Esther Rantzen, the founder of Childline, who during an interview gave me the courage to face my fear and shame. She said that 'It is never the child's fault it is always the abuser'. Those words were a source of strength to me as I finally realised that it wasn't my fault. How can a seven-year-old with all their innocence, be responsible for the abuser's actions? Accepting I was blameless was not enough; I needed to make changes and reclaim, all I had lost by discovering my true self, through connecting to my Inner Child.

This book was already written in journals and in my head. I now have an inner knowing that it is time to reach out and share my journey with you. I have worked in a caring environment, as a nurse—working with the homeless and alcoholics, later as a college lecturer, and for the past twenty-two years as a Colon Hydrotherapist. Throughout all my different roles I have been made aware that child sexual abuse is a hidden epidemic with destructive consequences, especially if it is allowed to continue and not addressed at the time. There is an accepted recognition that it can have long-term effect on health and wellbeing, as I can verify.

Since sharing my experience and leaving the previous edition of this book in the clinic, I have been overwhelmed by individuals who shared with me their personal experience of child sexual abuse and how they too have carried the shame and guilt for years but have never fully addressed the issue.

Although I have researched the subject of CSA for my own recovery and research for the book, this does not set me up as an authority on the subject. It is not, written by a "Guru", it is written from the heart, in an attempt to reach out and help you take the first step to find your true self.

Whilst we are all individuals who perceive things differently due to our individual personalities, I believe that through our shared experiences many of us react to situations in a similar way. Low self-esteem, lack of confidence, self-harm, un-warranted fears, to name but a few. We all have very different likes and dislikes. That is what makes us unique, but they can be rooted in a childhood memory. Prior to commencing my healing journey, I had a real dislike of parks; not one park in particular—all parks. It was something that I never questioned I just had an aversion to parks as they always made me feel anxious and irritable.

No, I wasn't sexually abused in a park as you might have been thinking. Parks had a strong association with my childhood, a place where I would spend time on my own with nowhere to go and nothing to do. It was only through working with my Inner Child the revelation came to me. Why do I act in certain ways? The answer lies in my childhood and the memories of my mother.

There are certain behaviour patterns that are more common amongst child sexual abuse victims, which may explain why you act and fear certain things, causing you to question why some seemingly easy tasks create such panic and dread.

There are many excellent books and support agencies that specialise in child sexual abuse. Many of the authors along with the founders of the support agencies have been victims themselves, they share their personal journeys and the strategies that have worked for them. The majority of the books follow a similar pattern, exploring the concepts of child sexual abuse, its implications, and the recovery phase working through a process of steps to initiate healing and the recommendation that you the victim seek help from one of the many support agencies through counselling and group support.

The majority of agencies involve interaction with others. Providing qualified counsellors to work with you on your healing journey. My book differs in that I am advocating that through commencing the self-help approach contained in this book you can start the process to heal yourself as I did, without the involvement of other people or agencies.

This is not to under mind the importance of counselling or any other therapies as a means of support and guidance.

There are many reasons why this may also be an option for you:

- It could be a time factor; you are too busy to attend support groups because of the demands of family and work.
- Financial implications involved in travel, counsellor's fees. Many of the support agencies do not charge for their services (but private counsellors do).
- Previous bad experience associated with taking people

into your confidence.

- Not wanting to divulge the details of the child sexual abuse at this point in time or to anyone.
- Curiosity using the self-help approach as a means of identifying if the abuse is responsible for your state of health and wellbeing.
- The shortage of counsellors available on the NHS resulting in long waiting times to access their services.

If the time is not right for you to fully COME OUT, by reading the book it is hoped that it will be a means of encouragement to take that first initial step however small.

This book has four parts:

Part One

Contains the bones of the child sexual abuse consisting of a short general background. How keeping sexual abuse, a secret is detrimental to health. The emotional trauma it inflicts on the victim. Identifying behaviour patterns that are common with adults who have been subjected to child sexual abuse. How the past is reflected in health and wellbeing. A questionnaire to assess how emotionally damaged victims may be. Case studies are included of historical sexual abuse.

Part Two

The main focus is on empowering you to embark on your own healing journey. I hope to achieve this by sharing my own personal journey from victim to thriver through a collection of stories and incidents related to my childhood. This will hopefully activate a desire to embrace the past and move forward as my personal journey demonstrates. Narcissistic Personality Disorder relating to my mother, is explained along with the effect of negative words. Twelve personality traits, allows you to assess your behaviour patterns and habits.

Part Three

"I am a child get me out of here" involves discovering your Inner Child, it contains practical activities to help you connect to, the frightened hurting child trapped within you. This is the initial key to learning to love yourself, which is crucial to your recovery. The need to forgive is also explored.

Part Four

This focuses on therapies that have been shown to promote recovery and the well-being of victims of child sexual abuse. All the therapies have been the tools for my healing. They include many therapies associated with energy:
Reiki, Sound Massage, Emotional Freedom Tapping, Flower Essence, Crystal Healing, Mirror Work, The Healing Codes and Ho'oponopno the latter are both forms of healing that involve releasing past negative thoughts and behaviour. Angel therapy and balancing the chakras are also discussed, along with the use of affirmations and meditation. The majority are stand-alone therapies that you can learn and implement yourself. The book also contains a framework for an Inner Child detox; if this Inner Child detox, is not an option you wish to embark upon, the book stands in its own right as a source of awareness and support. However, I strongly believe that we do need to cleanse and detox ourselves occasionally of acquired habits that no longer serve their purpose and benefit us now. We will work together in a truly holistic way throughout the recovery program in relation to body, mind, emotions and spirit.

I suggest that you initially read the book through once to get an overall picture of the book's intention. Make a mental note of topics or issues that speak directly to you, along with any activities or therapies you feel drawn to. Read the book a second time with added focus and carry out the various activities that you have selected. Continue to use the book as a point of reference and revisit for continued support and guidance.

Aims of the Book

- Provide you with the tools to discover your true self, by connecting to your Inner Child.
- Detach from the shame game associated with child sexual abuse.
- Discover appropriate ways of channelling your emotions and releasing inner stress and destructive cellular memories.
- Encourage you to leave your comfort zone and initiate change.
- Accepting that the past cannot be changed, but that you can create the future.
- Support you through your own personal healing journey.

What the book does not aim to do:

- Provide you with all the answers associated with your childhood.
- Just by reading the book, take away the pain and anger associated with the sexual abuse.
- Provide you with a quick fix program It demands a commitment and a genuine desire to initiate change.
- Protect you from the discomfort of starting to feel your pain and grief.
- Teach you how to feel good about yourself, only by learning to love yourself will that be achieved.
- Demand that you carry out any of the activities that don't resonate with you.
- Provide you with a guaranteed program for your recovery.

Whilst the whole purpose of writing the book is to reach out to the silent victims and to help them free themselves of the stigma of being a victim of child sexual abuse, the journey from victim to thriver can be a challenging one. It can cause you to experience flashbacks taking you back to dark places, which can last for hours, if not days whilst you work through the emotions. I can assure that there is light at the end of the tunnel. It is a process that needs to unfold as layers of hurt and pain surface. When this takes place, it is a sure sign that the wounds are deep, and the healing process has begun.

It is said that you cannot heal what you cannot feel. In other words, we need to connect and feel the pain associated with the memories in order to start the healing process.

Whilst writing this book there have been several occasions when I questioned why I was subjecting myself, to more hurt and pain. As I wrote about my childhood especially the relationship with my mother, it took me back to a dark place. I call this dark place the HELLISH HOLE. The hurt surfaced again, and I would find myself reliving the abuse and experiencing the pain. It would sometimes leave me feeling depressed. Thankfully through using some of my discovered coping techniques I am able to disconnect with the emotion quickly.

My commitment to you is to offer support as you activate your frozen feelings relating to sexual, physical or emotional abuse or any form of childhood abuse, which made you feel belittled or ignored. You may have learnt very early that it was not safe to feel. I want this book to create a safe haven for you where you can learn to connect to your feelings, let go of the past and learn to love yourself by acknowledging that you are worthy of love.

Please allow me to be your mentor, friend, colleague, and a source of strength. I hope that you will form a bond with me as you identify with my journey and consequently discover some tools to embark upon your own healing journey to freedom.

According to the presenters of an American talk show on ABC Television, "if a book is written from the heart the message will always get through". That is my ultimate aim, that the message will resonate within you and empower you to discover your true self.

Affirmations

Affirmations are simply statements that are said with confidence about a perceived truth.

Affirmations have helped many people make significant positive changes in their lives. They have the ability to program the mind into believing the stated concept. This is due to the mind not knowing the difference between what is real, and what is fantasy. There are both positive and negative types of affirmations. During childhood negative statements have an impact on development, negative statements can remain locked in to both our conscious and unconscious mind. It is believed that the lack of one or both parent's positive affirmation leaves some children emotionally crippled.

You are what you eat

To me "You are what you eat" is more than a hackneyed saying; it's reality, demonstrated by working daily with people whose health has deteriorated due to unhealthy food choices. Whatever the reason the result is the same, the body is out of balance especially in relation to the digestive system, resulting in failing health.

Whilst I truly believe in the philosophy it is outshined by another revelation YOU ARE WHAT YOU THINK. Negative thoughts lead to negative behaviour. One of my healing tools is the daily practice of saying affirmations to change my thought patterns.

With this in mind, throughout the book I have used some of the positive affirmations as both titles of chapters and headings. They have been selected over the years from Louise Hay affirmation calendars entitled YOU CAN DO IT.

All is well, and even better things are coming—Louise Hay

Part One

The Statistics

"Child sexual abuse in the UK is a national epidemic"— Graham Wilmer, founder of the Lantern Project

A child is sexually abused when they are forced or persuaded to take part in sexual activities. This does not have to be physical contact, and it can happen online. Sometimes the child won't understand that what's happening to them is abuse. They may not even understand that it's wrong. (NSPCC 2014.)

The problem with associating CSA with statistics is that they are nothing more than a piece of data. Statistics are facts and figures that can only give you an estimated measurement of the extent of CSA. Whilst the following statistics may be alarming, they do not have a voice; they cannot convey the trauma and the emotional pain that is inflicted on its young victims.

- 1 in 20 children in the UK have been sexually abused NSPCC 2017
- 1 in 3 children sexually abused never tell anyone at the time (Cawson et al. 2000)
- 90% of victims, were abused by someone they knew
- 16% of Police recorded child sexual offences involved online elements in England and Wales. April 2015 ONS. Gov.
- 73,518 offenses including online grooming and sexual assault against children in the UK in 2019/20, up by 57% in five years since 2014/15 - Childline
- Over 8,000 contacts to NSPCC helpline in 2017/18 were concerns about sexual abuse.

Government Statistics state that CSA in those under 16 involve one in four girls and one in six boys.

A report between 2012 and 2014 conducted by Anne Langfield, the Children's Commissioner for England, revealed that 425,000 children had encountered sexual abuse.

This equates to within any town of 100.000 in population 800 children have experienced sexual abuse.

The study involved the police, social services and voluntary organisations. The main findings revealed that two thirds of the abusers are known to the family.

When an incident of abuse was reported, 21% of the reported abuse stopped, whilst in 18%, the victim was punished, and the situation got worse.

Disabled children are three times more likely to become victims than non-disabled children.

Children tell up to six times before they are believed.

In 75% of cases no conviction is granted.

The above data was presented in a documentary entitled *The Truth about Child Sexual Abuse*, screened on BBC2 on the 24th, November 2015.

Thankfully there are now more than 130 groups offering support to victims of sexual abuse in the UK and they work under the network of the Survivors Trust. One such group is the Lantern Project. Its founder Graham Wilmer told Sky News that potentially there are another 11.7 million victims out there at the moment, who have not been disclosed. Childline is a child help line, which works with victims of sexual abuse, founded in 1986 by Dame Esther Rantzen. It provides a 24-hour counselling service for children up to their 19th birthday in the UK.

When you consider that the RSPCA (Royal Society Prevention of Cruelty to Animals) was founded in 1824, whilst the NSPCC (National Society Prevention Cruelty to Children) was not founded until 1884 sixty years later, it is a clear indicator why child sexual abuse has been allowed to flourish.

Whilst using statistics as the core measurement of how society engages with the epidemic of child sexual abuse, we cannot say they are an accurate estimation of the extent of child sexual abuse. No sooner have the latest statistics been released than they quickly become outdated as evidence of new cases are uncovered.

Initially I started to gather information regarding child sexual abuse from newspapers and support agencies, which gave me the impetus to continue to complete my book as it confirmed my belief of how widespread historical child sexual abuse is. However due to the constant amount of information that is being generated by the media it became impossible to keep updated with the current situation in relation to individual cases and statistical evidence.

Rogues' Gallery

Never before in history has there been so much awareness of sexual abuse. The media is constantly highlighting renowned celebrities associated with sexual abuse. These crimes often date back many years and the majority of them involve children as their victims. They include Gary Glitter, Dave Lee Travis, Max Clifford, Rolf Harris, Stuart Hall, Chris Denning, Michael Salmon and Fred Talbot. David Smith was under investigation he worked for the BBC and committed suicide the day of his trial. Cyril Smith MP for Rochdale was also under investigation but was never formally charged.

Operation Yew Tree is a police enquiry started in October 2012, which led to 400 lines of enquiry relating to Jimmy Savile following his death in 2011. The enquiry concluded that whilst never charged or convicted, Jimmy Savile, was deemed to be a predatory sex offender – probably one of Britain's most prolific. There had been allegations during his lifetime, but they were dismissed, and accusers ignored or disbelieved. This action proved to be a catalyst for a change. By exposing him it changed attitudes towards sexual abuse, as the details of his activities unfolded. Many people initially defended him questioning the accuracy of the evidence. It did however give everyone the opportunity to express an opinion on the taboo subject of child sexual abuse. This ignited the debate and set the stage for other victims to come forward.

Following widespread national publicity regarding historical, not recent, child sexual abuse in football, many police forces throughout the country continue to receive calls from both victims and people offering information relating to child sexual abuse.

The information is collated by Operation Hydrant. This is a British police investigation into allegations of non-recent sexual abuse, headed by Simon Bailey the Chief Constable of Norfolk. In June 2016 there were 2,777 suspects in the database. Operation Hydrant acts an interface between the police and the independent enquiry into child sexual abuse. Ninety-eight football clubs were under investigation, ranging from the Premier League through to the amateur leagues.

One club Crewe Alexandra, employed Barry Bennell as their youth coach in the 1980s. He was eventually jailed for nine years in 1998 after admitting abusing boys as young as nine. In 2015 Barry Bennell was given a further two years for another historical sexual offence against a 12 year old boy. As of December 2017, the official overall Operation Hydrant statistics shows that there were 2,094 cases of historical child sexual abuse under investigation, this compares with 1,433 in May 2015. This reinforces the argument that we have only just begun to uncover the true extent of historical child sexual abuse. Gender is of no significance; all children are potentially at risk of being violated.

The Rochdale child sexual abuse scandal involved under-age teenage girls being raped and used in sexual trafficking. Forty-seven girls were identified as victims of child sexual abuse. In March 2015 Greater Manchester Police apologised for its failure to investigate the child sexual allegations more thoroughly. It was alleged the failure to investigate claims was due to the fear of being accused of racism.

Another report revealed that at least 1,400 children were subjected to sexual exploitation in Rotherham between 1997 and 2013. "Children as young as 11 were raped by multiple perpetrators, abducted, beaten and intimated".

It will only be when statistics raise their voice that the true picture will emerge. One such courageous individual was ex footballer Andrew Woodward who waived his right to anonymity when he disclosed the sexual abuse, he had endured by Barry Bennell for four years at Crewe Alexandra. He spoke openly on the BBC Victoria Derbyshire morning program of how his life had been ruined as he lived in torment even coming close to suicide on several occasions. His coming out was the impetus for many other victims to come forward.

Silent Statistic Keeping a Big Secret

Statistical data reveals that one in three sexual acts against children are never reported.

With over 130 support agencies in the UK the question needs to be asked: With so much help and support available why do one in three victims choose to keep it a secret and never tell anyone? However, it is not guaranteed that if you share your secret with others, you will be believed, as I discovered when I attempted to make the abuse stop by telling my mother and auntie. When I was 13 years old, I also told a church youth leader, they responded in three different ways.

Auntie Alice

I would have been around nine when I told her that my uncle was making me do things I didn't want to do. I used to go to their house every Friday straight from school for my tea. He would then walk me back home and babysit whilst my mother went out. My father would have already left to go to work as a barman.

My auntie appeared not to believe me; she said that my uncle loved me and that he would do anything for me. She reminded me that he had bought me dolls and books.

The following week walking back home he asked me why I had told my auntie and how upset she was when I had told her about our secret. He then recalled an incident where I along with some other children had climbed on to a steamroller that had been left over the weekend on some spare land near to the house. I fell from the vehicle and broke my arm. I lied to my mother as to how the accident happened telling her I had slipped on some leaves. I am not sure how my uncle knew the truth; had he seen it happen or had heard me discussing it with friends or my brother? The fact was he had a weapon to use against me, which silenced me. I never told my auntie again. As I am recalling the incident I question if she did believe me but the consequences of speaking out were too great. Prior to me telling her about the abuse I remember sleeping in the same bed as them, I would sleep in the middle of the bed. The sleeping arrangements then changed. Auntie Alice started to sleep in the middle with us either side of her.

My Mother

I told my mother twice about the abuse, the first time I would have been about eight, I think. She did believe me as she stopped him from coming to babysit for several weeks. I was not allowed to go to their house after school. At the time she said that if I told my father, she would kill me. My mother often used physical violence against me, so the threat of a beating was enough to silence me on that occasion.

My mother staying home with us on a Friday evening didn't last many weeks as her need to see her new boyfriend was greater than protecting me. I had seen her getting out of a van one Friday night my uncle was babysitting. The man she was seeing was the man she eventually married.

The second time I told her was not to protect myself but my younger sister. To try and avoid him on a Friday night I would play out late even when it was dark (that's how I had seen my mother getting out of a van). My younger sister asked me not to play out and to go to bed with her, as she didn't like our uncle. She would have been four at the time and I would have been ten. She explained that he came into our bedroom. When I told my mother the following day, she didn't ask any questions about the incident.

The following Friday evening when I returned with my uncle, she verbally challenged him and ordered him to get out the house. He denied it all saying it was all a lie on my behalf.

I'm not sure when, but I do recall my mother and me going to visit my auntie when my uncle was not there. She told her about the sexual abuse. I remember my auntie crying and I was forbidden from visiting their home again. It was on the way home that my mother first called me a dirty bitch. She was probably annoyed that she would not be able to sneak out on a Friday night. My mother said that I had blackmailed him. I did not know what blackmailing was. She referred to the dolls and books he and my auntie had bought me. She said I was always threatening to tell my dad if he didn't buy me gifts. Throughout my childhood my mother would often refer to me as a 'dirty bitch'. The sad thing was, I believed her.

A Church Youth Leader

When I was 14 years old, I told a youth leader about my childhood experience. Unfortunately, she shared the information with her fiancé who told others within the church. This resulted in three men asking me outright if this was true. The consequence of betraying my trust was the reason I never sought counselling and embarked upon a self-healing program.

A question for you

Read through the list below which; category relates to you? Are you someone who:
- Is still struggling with the stigma of the sexual abuse
- Has successfully put the past behind them and has moved on
- Has never received any form of therapy
- Spoke out and brought the offender to justice
- Reported the incident but was shamed and humiliated
- Was not believed
- Was believed but was not protected from the abuser
- Never told, anyone?

If this is you it may be the time to stop being a silent statistic with no voice, the fact that you are reading this book is perhaps an indicator that the silence has started to break.

Keeping a Secret

From the age of 14, due to the negative response I received from the three people I chose to share my secret with, I never told my childhood secret to anyone. I only shared it with my husband after we had been married several years. My coping mechanism was to detach from anything associated with child sexual abuse in an attempt to avoid taking me to that dark place where the guilt and shame would surface. The guilt and shame were constantly reinforced by my mother's cruel words over the years, as she continued to call me a dirty bitch when I didn't meet her demands.

It is well documented that keeping a secret is also detrimental to health. According to Gina Roberts Grey. Keeping secrets and not having the opportunity to confess and share our secrets causes multiple health issues. These include stress, hypertension, digestive problems, impacting on memory, insomnia, problems with metabolism causing weight issues, reduced immunity, mood swings, and depression.

According to Alcoholics Anonymous you are only as sick as your secret.

Neuroscientists have basically discovered that within the human brain the Cingulate Cortex is wired to tell the truth. When this is denied by keeping silent, the stress hormone cortisol is produced, which puts the body into the flight or fight mode. When this response is turned on for too long it becomes toxic in the body and contributes to an array of health problems. They conclude that the bigger the secret the more impact it has on health.

This was verified in a famous study by Adverse Childhood Experience (ACE), which is now used within the USA, Canada and some places in Europe as a tool to identify victims of child abuse and links to chronic health issues and behaviour traits. The study also concluded that victims were 12 times more likely to have attempted suicide than those who had no adverse experiences in childhood. Another study revealed that eating disorders are common amongst adult survivors of child abuse.

In 1985 Vincent Fellitti was frustrated as to why his patients who were achieving great results for their obesity problems quit his program when they were losing weight. He interviewed around two hundred dropouts from the program. One of the structured questions asked, "How much did you weigh when you became sexually active?" The revelation came when a female patient answered 'Forty pounds. It was when I was four years old, with my father". The study was extended and of 286 people interviewed most had been sexually abused as children. It was found that obesity was used in the same way as alcohol, tobacco and drugs. It helped fix a problem. Whilst over-eating soothed their anxiety and depression it also gave them a sense of protection as in the case of a female rape victim who believed that by being overweight, she was unattractive and invisible and therefore would not be at risk from future molesting. She believed being obese protected her. Similarly, a male who was abused as a skinny child gained weight in later years as he too thought it would protect him. By losing weight they perceived themselves as targets again which increased anxiety, depression and fear levels.

Further studies were undertaken in the 90s. The data revealed beyond doubt that childhood trauma has a direct link to chronic disease as well as mental illness, spending time in prison, work issues and absenteeism. Adults with a history of child abuse and neglect are more likely to experience physical health problems including diabetes, gastrointestinal problems, stroke, hepatitis and heart disease; this was the findings of (Fellitti et al 1998.

According to Adverse Childhood Experience those who have an alcoholic father are more likely to have encountered physical or verbal abuse. This revealed that adverse child experiences don't happen in isolation. A scoring chart was created and those with an elevated score are more likely to be violent, to experience more broken marriages, take more prescribed drugs, suffer with depression, encounter more auto immune disease and more work absences.

There is also a correlation between mental health problems associated with past CSA and neglect. They include personality disorders post-traumatic stress disorders, depression, anxiety disorders and psychosis (Cannon et al 2010)

Apart from the emotional issues I experienced I have also suffered with quite a few health issues over the years. As a child I suffered with multiple ear and sinuses problems. On my journey of recovery, I became aware of the correlation between health issues and emotional baggage that we carry deep within our cellular memory. This revelation was through reading Louise Hay's book *You Can Heal Your Life.* Louise was a victim of child sexual abuse herself and has written many books, which I will discuss in detail in Part Four. In her book and to my amazement, she claims sinuses and ear problems are caused by living in a house where there is constant tension and arguments.

Myths Relating to Child Sexual Abuse

One of the major elements in dealing with the child sexual abuse is the amount of support you are given from your parents. This is not always available, and many victims are subjected to a barrage of lies from their perpetrator, family and society, which only adds more misery and suffering for the victims.

The perpetrator may say that it is alright to have sex with children as a way of teaching them about sex and the act is a way of showing the child how much they love and care for them and they are special.

The family may also lie to the child by saying that the abuse didn't exist, and that the child had made it up or it didn't cause any harm and was just a way of showing affection, playing down the event and putting the guilt on to the child

Society is also responsible for covering up the extent of the problem by not being pro-active in the past to the plight of the victims. The deceit is detrimental to victims as it adds to the confusion and bewilderment of how to deal with the abuse causing them to in some cases deny the abuse ever took place, which keeps them trapped in the shame game and anchored to the past.

As I previously mentioned, when I was living with my dark secret, each time there was a reference to child sexual abuse on the television I would either go out of the room or change the channel, avoiding the many painful memories from flooding back. At that point I chose to suppress them.

I clearly remember many years ago sitting through a class in college when the subject of child sexual abuse was being discussed by an outside speaker. Two students left the class during the lecture, as it was too difficult for them to remain. I on the other hand remained throughout. Not able to listen, I sat there humming under my breath. I saw it as a challenge that my past had no claim on me, I was so proud of myself. I couldn't share my triumph with anyone. What does that tell me now? I was in total denial despite the effect it was having on me.

A question for you

So how do you react to the topic of sexual abuse when it is discussed, or you are confronted with it via the media? Do you remain silent and distance yourself from it by switching your focus to something else? Do you play it down? Perhaps rationalising that it happens to many others so it's no big deal? Whatever your coping mechanisms, does it really stop that deep inner hurt that you were an innocent child who was violated by someone to fulfil their sexual needs?

Become aware of how your body reacts to the words, "sexual abuse"; what effect does it have on you physically? Do you feel uncomfortable even vocalising the words "child sexual abuse"? Can you feel your body go tense? Does your heartbeat louder? I believe this is negative energy that has built up over the years and has been suppressed, words evoke strong emotions. I would like you to become aware, as you read through the book, how your body reacts to the written word and how it makes you feel. I suggest that it will cause a physical and emotional negative reaction if you are still seeing yourself as a victim and not a thriver. The way you respond physically and emotionally is an indicator as to how the abuse is responsible for your present state of mind. Unfortunately, we do not listen to our bodies; if we only could relearn how to connect with our inner being we would discover how to live, in harmony and have a more fulfilling life.

When The Past Dictates Your Future

How can you spot another victim of child sexual abuse? It is impossible unless you are in a therapy group. There is a consensus amongst the support agencies that certain characteristics are prominent amongst victims. During my recovery phase I read many books relating to Inner Child work and dysfunctional families. I was amazed to discover that many of my behaviour traits are the result of my childhood abuse.

Whilst it could be said that I have achieved so much considering my starting post which I will share in Part Two, here it is enough to say that my childhood was not easy, and I guess many of you also had a very difficult childhood. There are certain things I react to that are not rational. If I ever accidentally break anything I start to shake and stammer. My adult self knows this reaction is not appropriate, but I have no control over it. I revert to a child as the memory of the consequences of breaking something would result in a beating and severe punishment, not only from my mother but sometimes also my father when he returned from work as my mother would embellish the incident by making it out I did it deliberately. It was often the emotional stress that was more traumatic than the initial beating.

Another thing I came across, children, who have been neglected not necessarily physically, but emotionally, exhibit certain marked characteristics. I am very fearful about driving, which is no big deal, many people don't enjoy driving seeing it as a necessity rather than a pleasure. For me, it is more than that; I constantly feel intimidated by drivers who drive right up to me and push me to break the speed limit and go faster. If I look at their face, they appear angry and annoyed at me, which presents me with a dilemma? Do I go faster to please them and run the risk of breaking the law, which would result in putting me under more pressure? It sounds crazy even now typing the words. Another issue I have regarding the car is putting petrol in. I get so anxious about doing it, imagine my surprise when I read in a book that this is a common trait for victims of CSA.

To be honest I do still have a few behaviour issues that I need to address and work through despite the fact that I have come a long way in my journey of discovery. Life is a challenge, as the saying goes. No pain no gain. Addressing issues relating to CSA is not easy as you will discover but the past is instrumental in creating your future for good or bad. Going back to my reaction to breaking something, the memory has been stored at a cellular level, on its own automatic program response. In the same context your past could also be dictating both your present and future.

To assist you in discovering more about yourself I have formulated a questionnaire. It's modified from John Bradshaw's book, *Homecoming: Reclaiming and Championing Your Inner Child* and also Charles L Whitefield's, *Healing the Inner Child* along with some of my questions relating to an assessment of my own behaviour traits. The questionnaire is primarily formulated for victims of sexual abuse; however, it is acknowledged that it may also be relevant to anyone who considers themselves to be a victim of a dysfunctional family. Please try and answer the questions as honestly as you can.

How Emotionally Challenged am I?

- Do you have feelings of shame regarding your experience of child sexual abuse?
- Do you find it difficult to make decisions?
- Do you constantly seek the approval of others?
- Do you consider the needs of others more important than your own?
- Do you find it difficult to relax and have fun?
- Do you have a strong work ethic?
- Are you a perfectionist?
- Is it difficult to laugh from the heart?
- Do you find it difficult to cry?
- Have you suffered or are suffering with depression?
- Do you feel empty and numb of emotion?
- Did you have an unhappy childhood?
- Are there more unhappy childhood memories than happy ones?
- Did you suffer rejection as a child?
- Do you still find it difficult to cope with rejection?
- Do you feel that siblings were treated different to you?
- Do you suffer from low self-esteem?
- Are you fearful of the future?
- Have you suffered from any addictions or eating problems?
- Do you have any chronic health problems?
- Do you find it hard to trust people?
- Do you feel that people take advantage of you?
- Are you afraid of taking a challenge?
- Do you isolate yourself from other people?

If you have answered yes to the majority of the questions it strongly indicates that the consequences of your childhood are a barrier to discovering your true self and allowing you to lead a more balanced and creative life. However, answering yes to the majority of the questions does not indicate that you have been sexually abused

Another exercise that will highlight the possibility that your childhood is still having an effect on you is to look at the two lists below, select six words that best describe you.

Positive:

Happy, secure, fulfilled, optimistic, loved, in control, focused, content, blessed, peaceful, energised, accepted, confident, balanced, strong.

Negative:

Angry, anxious, fearful, unhappy, hurting, rejected, unloved, confused, insecure, suspicious, numb, drained, irritable, useless, stupid.

Ideally your list should contain more positive feelings than negative. I suspect for many of you this will not be the case. You have to feel secure and in control and value yourself. The past is so influential at dictating your future, as you remain a victim of your childhood.

The whole concept of personality traits and behaviour patterns will be explored in Part Three when you consider and hopefully connect to your Inner Child.

How The Past Can Dictate the Future

Through my own experience and working with the homeless, along with my role as a nurse, lecturer and a therapist, I have heard so many similar stories to my own; different in content, but all share a common bond through identifying with the negative emotions and issues associated with our childhood sexual abuse.

The case studies below are a mixture of both factual and fictional characters in an attempt to conceal their true identity. The common thread is that all are hurting individuals who have shared with me their stories of child sexual abuse including in some cases neglect and emotional abuse. Several have never told anyone about their abuse and consequently have received no professional help. One thing they all have in common is the guilt and shame they continued to carry. This can manifest into self-disgust, which is anchored deep within the sub conscious mind and has never had the opportunity or the means of being addressed and then worked upon. This can result in victims not being able to fulfil their full potential caused by neglecting a basic need to love themselves.

Their stories stirred such a deep dark place within me as I listened. But whilst I could empathise, I never shared my secret with the majority of them. I can only imagine that I was locked into my feelings of shame and my decision not to share my past was my coping strategy at the time.

Case Studies

Margaret

Repeatedly raped by her stepfather from the age of 14 years and pregnant at 15 years.

Baby adopted. Married at 18 years. Had three children who were taken into care. Had a history of mental illness and self-harm.

Margaret was a 56 year's old lady who I met when I worked with the homeless in 1983. She was suffering from mental illness and was known to self-harm on more than one occasion whilst living at the homeless centre. After returning from the hospital after taking an overdose. On her return to the hostel, she shared with me her challenging past.

Whilst I knew that she was diagnosed with a personality disorder and had to take large amounts of medication to keep her stable, I had never questioned what had led her to become so dependent on medication to help her function. She shared with me how she had no family to call her own, that she had given birth to three children and had no contact with any of them.

Margaret had been repeatedly raped by her stepfather from the age of 14 years. Her biological father had left her and her mother and younger brother when she was ten. Her stepfather turned out to be a violent man who would become violent towards her mother when he had had too much alcohol. On one occasion she remembers that when she tried to run out of the house to avoid his advances, he beat her with a leather strap across her buttocks and then raped her on the kitchen table whilst her mother and younger brother were upstairs. To keep her from screaming he held a towel over her mouth. She became pregnant at the age of 15, she was too afraid to tell her mother about her stepfather I presumed she was too sacred of the consequences if she told the truth.

She talked of how things changed once it was generally known of her condition, her best friend was not allowed to speak to her, and she was taunted and called abusive names by neighbours. She was sent to a mother and baby home in Liverpool where she gave birth to a baby boy, which was adopted.

Margaret married at 18 to an abusive husband who had both a drink and gambling problem. He couldn't hold a job down and so she had to work to provide for his drinking habits. When she became pregnant again there were complications, which resulted in her taking time off work, this caused the loss of her job in the textile mill.

Following the birth of her baby boy she could not work, having no family to help her with the baby. It was at this time that Margaret became unwell suffering with depression. Her husband became more violent towards her as she was unable to cope with the pressure of looking after the baby. She neglected both the baby and herself. The baby boy was undernourished and Social Services became involved. Eventually she was admitted to hospital and the baby taken into care.

When she was discharged several months later, she went to live in a hostel. Her husband had left the family home and the baby was with foster parents. Her husband had disappeared with no trace. She was eventually reunited with her son and was found council accommodation. She was struggling again with depression as she tried to take care of her son. She tried to commit suicide and was admitted to hospital. She was given ECT and remained in a mental hospital for almost three years. When she was discharged, she went to live in a bedsit. Whilst in hospital she had met a man who was a schizophrenic who later moved in with her.

Within two years she was back in hospital and pregnant again. Margaret has little memory of these difficult months. Her new partner stopped taking his medication and encouraged her to do the same. He became paranoid, not letting her leave the house, at one point he locked her in the bedroom for two days. She escaped by smashing the bedroom window, which brought it to the attention of the neighbours.

He was eventually sectioned again, and she was admitted to a different hospital in another town. The baby, another boy, was also placed into care and was eventually adopted.

Margaret had lived at the centre for homeless people for several years. Apart from visits from the mental health team she received no visitors. On good days she would venture out into town but the majority of time she stayed in her room.

I saw her as a hurting, wounded individual who was on a self-sabotage mission. Haunted by memories, she battled alone needing to take the medication to numb the emotional pain, which prevents her from addressing the past and its consequences. Margaret had no love for herself. If I had known then what I know now, I feel I may have been able to help Margaret more. Whilst I could never have taken the pain away for her, perhaps if I had shared my story of sexual abuse, she may then have been able to trust me more and taken practical steps to place the past behind her and move on.

Carla

Sexually abused by her father. Sent to live with her maternal grandparents at the age of 13.

Carla lived at the centre too, she came across as being self-assured and confident—the opposite to Margaret. She was brought to the centre by the police due to being a witness in a drug incident in a large city and her life had been threatened. She was initially hostile to the management staff saluting us when we walked past her. I remember one night she had returned to the centre late in a drunken state and I was called across to deal with the situation. I had no choice but to leave her outside as she was throwing bricks at the window and hurling abuse. I told security that she could not come in until she was sober. That night I could not sleep worrying about her, what if she was knocked down by a car or was beaten up by the pimps who frequented the streets around the centre.

It later transpired that she had one of the other female residents come down to a ground floor window and open it for her to get in. I didn't discover this until months later.

Eventually Carla settled into the centre and became less disruptive to staff and other residents. She was eventually asked to take on a position of working in the kitchen as a kitchen porter. It was during this time, she shared with me her past regarding her father's sexual advances and how she was moved to live with her grandparents.

There was now no contact with her mother or father, who had owned several residential homes. As she told me she started to cry, which was so out of character as she came across as being so strong and in control. She explained that she had told her mother about the sexual abuse but was not believed; her father denied it. Whilst he never touched her again after the confrontation, she felt that both her parents started to treat her differently compared to her younger brother and sister. Over the years her schoolwork declined, she started mixing with what can only be described as the wrong crowd. She started smoking and drinking along with petty theft, which was the gang's initiation test. She began bunking off school and was eventually caught shop lifting with the others in a department store.

At the age of 14 years, she was sent to Swindon to live with her grandparents. She was soon involved with another gang, which involved prostitution. She was only 15 years when she had sex with someone for money as a dare. Eventually the gang leader became her pimp. She started smoking cannabis and taking what I presumed were highs. She continued to live with her grandparents, but she admitted they couldn't cope with her behaviour. She was eventually sent to a detention centre for two years. On release she returned to live with her grandparents. Whilst in the detention centre and later at her grandparents, she was only visited by her mother and younger sister. On release within a few months, she became involved with the same gang and left her grandparents and started living in a squat. It was whilst living in the squat that she started taking drugs again. After several months she was arrested. This was the result of a police raid following a stabbing in the town, drugs and stolen goods were found and many arrests were made, including Carla.

Whilst in custody Carla divulged names and details of the drug suppliers and dates of alleged crimes and those involved. This resulted in threats to her life and a physical attack with a knife, inflicting stab wounds and a long gash in both of her arms and back. I first met Carla when she was brought to the centre by the police to stay with us until after the court appearance when the gang was eventually convicted. Carla stayed at the centre and embarked on a college course studying aspects of social care. This enabled her to work in the care environment. She eventually left the centre and started working with vulnerable teenage girls.

Elaine

Raped by her brother's best friend whilst she was still at school.

History of depression.

I also met Elaine whist working with the homeless. I didn't know her for long as she stayed with us for only a few weeks. During that time, I discovered that she had been raped by her brother's best friend whilst she was still at school and had had an abortion.

I can only imagine the trauma that must have caused her. She shared this with me as she was now 19 years old and pregnant again and due to her chronic depression and lack of support, she felt under pressure to have another abortion. I don't know the outcome to Elaine's plight as she and her boyfriend one day just disappeared from the centre.

Linda

> *Sexually abused by a youth leader when she was 15, which continued for several months. It came to an end when they were seen in his car by his wife.*

I met Linda through coming to the clinic, over a period of several years. Her health was fragile, she had been diagnosed with M.E. several years ago. She had many food intolerances, causing her to have a restricted diet. She was very timid, constantly apologising without any reason to do so. Physically she fluctuated according to the seasons and her eating regime. Emotionally she was a wreck; she had no self-esteem, and was in a long-term relationship, which provided no support. She had one son who was at university.

Following an emotional healing session, she shared her past, which involved being sexually abused by a youth club leader when she was 15 years old. He would run her home after the meeting, buy her small gifts, tell her how unhappy he was with his marriage. He had a daughter who was 12 years at the time who was in Linda's guide patrol.

One night he had taken her to a layby after youth club when a church elder and his wife approached the car, and they were caught together. The consequence was that he eventually moved away with his family.

Linda remembers the change of attitude towards her from her parents, especially her mother, along with some church people. This resulted in her stopping going to church and loosing contact with several friends. She was offered no official counselling or support. The incident was never discussed with her parents. Several years later due to her poor health state her doctor had recommended a course of counselling. During a counselling session she revealed her past. Unfortunately, due to funding, she was only allocated six sessions. Incidentally Linda was the first person in a work situation that I shared my secret with. I feel it gave her a sense of security and enabled to work on the trauma of the past and to address the guilt and shame that she continued to carry all these years later.

Anne

Sexually abused by a neighbour when she used to babysit for him and his wife. Resulted in having to move from the area as he denied it and told his wife and other neighbours that she was the one who made advances towards him.

I met Anne through coming to the clinic for colonic treatments, due to issues with digestion. Having undergone several tests nothing had been detected, she was given the diagnosis of Irritable Bowel Syndrome (IBS) Her symptoms could be extreme, often resulting in excruciating pain in her abdomen. She found her job very demanding, which resulted in her being away from home during the week and doing lot of traveling, sometimes in Europe. She had two children.

During a session she shared that she and her husband were not getting along, and the tension was making her symptoms worse. She felt they had simply grown apart as they never did anything together as a family. We talked about her job situation and the need to make some changes. She shared some childhood experiences, which included a situation when, she was attacked by a neighbour who was walking her home after she had been babysitting for him and his wife.

He had pushed her against a wall and grabbed her breasts putting his knee in her groin, she had screamed, and he stopped. Her father made her go to the house with him and confront him along with his wife. It was denied by both of them. She felt that her father thought she had made more of the ordeal by the fact that she didn't tell her parents straight away.

The outcome was several other people got involved. Hurtfully she was called a slut by a group of teenage boys one day at the bus stop. A shopkeeper's wife asked her if it was true and what had happened. On one occasion the abuser's wife also called her a name as she passed her on the street.

It eventually made her family leave the area and relocate. This caused a lot of friction for her family along with financial problems. She and her brother had to change schools, which was a difficult time for them both. Anne believed that she was part responsible for her parents eventually getting divorced. I cannot conclude that the sexual encounter with the neighbour is the sole cause of her health issues. But I am confident due to my own past experience that many health problems are rooted in cellular memories, which manifest in emotional stress and consequent health issues.

Caroline

Sexually abused by a shopkeeper when she was 16. He used to pick her up after work and take her home. The case went to court, but he was acquitted through lack of evidence.

Caroline was deputy head of a primary school. She attended the clinic regularly due to chronic constipation along with severe eczema and food intolerances.

At the time when I knew her, she was having an affair with a married colleague who had two young children. This was adding to her stress levels causing her general health to decline. The affair was not generally known within the school, so her treatments included lots of discussion concerning her male work colleague, who she loved to talk about. I think in a way this was to gain my approval of the affair. Whilst discussing his children and how they would cope if he left his wife and moved in with her, she revealed that she had once been placed into the care of Social Services along with her younger sister due to her father sexually abusing her when she was around eight. They were eventually placed back into the care of their mother. She saw her father only on supervised visits until she was 12 when he then disappeared. There has been no contact with him since. On one occasion her mother had said she didn't believe that their father had sexually assaulted her and that she was a liar and had been responsible for breaking up the marriage.

She made her recall some of the times that her father had made advances, which generally focused on bath time. Her mother had said that her father was only drying her properly. She said the fact that her mother did not believe her, plus her being accused of breaking up her parent's marriage, was as traumatic as the actual sexual abuse she encountered from her father.

Helen

Raped by a cousin when she was 15 years now suffers with stress and panic attacks.

Helen was a workaholic, the head teacher of, a primary school. She came to see me for stress management, which involved aromatherapy massage and reflexology. She was on long term sick, experiencing panic attacks, which she felt was triggered by a recent OFSTED inspection. She was also experiencing difficulties within her marriage and her mother had suddenly died the previous year. Her father's health was also a concern at that time. He did not live locally, which was another area of stress, as she felt the need to visit weekly and this involved a round trip of 200 miles. She was the only child.

Over a period of many months, she gradually took control of the situation and returned to work but still came for treatments once a month. I got to know Helen quite well and several times after a session she would stay and share a meal with me.

It was during a meal that she told me she had been raped by her cousin in her bedroom, whilst the rest of the family were downstairs. He was 17 and she was nearly 15. She never told her parents of the incident. Whilst it only happened once, she had lived with guilt and the shame she associated with the abuse. She now only sees her cousin occasionally at family gatherings as he lives in London and is married with children. Helen made a point of me knowing that I was the only person she had ever shared her secret with.

I feel that it was through sharing with her my childhood experiences and telling her I was writing this book that enabled her to share with me her childhood sexual experience. Whilst you cannot make any claims that health issues have any links to sexual abuse, nor can you deny that the stress that Helen encountered was deep rooted in her psyche, which resulted from her cousin's sexual attack.

The above only presents the bare facts of the individual's story. They do not portray the full impact the sexual abuse has on the victims in relation to physical, mental, emotional and spiritual health.

I accept everyone as they are, including myself—Louise Hay

Whilst recalling my encounters with the above case studies, it gives me a sense of belonging and motivation to complete this book. So easily I can allow myself to slip back into feeling marginalised as feelings of anxiety can surface, as I feel others may still judge me and blame me for my past. I am motivated by the fact that there are so many hurting victims living with the shame and guilt they enforce upon themselves. I relate to the words of Andrew Woodward the ex. footballer, "Only now at the age of 43, I feel I can actually live without that secret…..I want to get it out and give other people an opportunity to do the same".

Hopefully you will have been able to relate to other victim's stories and have developed a sense of belonging along with a desire to make plans for your own journey of recovery.

If you are still unsure if you are ready to address some of the issues involved, Part Two may give you the stimulus to let go of the hold the past has over you and find your true self. Our childhood becomes the blueprint for our future, which becomes more evident in Part Three when we consider the role of our Inner Child.

I was once asked who hurt me the most, my uncle or my mother. There is no doubt it was my mother. As my story unfolds in Part Two you will hopefully understand why. There is a saying that sticks and stones may break my bones but calling names won't hurt me. This childhood chant is simply not true as the words 'dirty bitch' were anchored so deep within me that I believed that I was unworthy of being loved.

Part Two

Chart the Course

I honestly cannot recall many happy memories relating to my childhood, the few that I do remember were not associated with my immediate family and home. I was always happier at my grandma and grandad's house or church. I was not happy at home or school, where I was the target of bullying at both primary and secondary school. In retrospect I can now understand why. Being so withdrawn, along with the condition of the clothes I was made to wear, made me a target for bullies. Having endured bullying as a child I was able to use the experiences in a positive way several years later by carrying out research within further education. This resulted in writing an anti-bullying policy, which was adopted and used as a framework for further research into bullying. Importantly it brought an awareness of the problem, and some tutors used the policy as part of group tutorials, which hopefully resulted in a decrease of bullying incidents throughout college. In a similar way I hope that through my personal experience of sexual abuse I can turn the negative into positive by sharing my journey with you, which will hopefully empower you to commence your own healing journey.

Child sexual abuse and bullying share common ground. The victims especially in my generation had no voice. There were no help lines or guidelines for victims of child sexual abuse or anti bullying policies within schools. In both child sexual abuse and bullying it was evident, it was obvious, and it was allowed to exist as the numerous enquiries have proved in relation to child sexual abuse. Some authorities appeared to have spent time and resources covering up and protecting the guilty at the cost to the true victims.

The primary aim of all the stories that I have written regarding my childhood memories are to give you an insight into some of the complex situations my childhood produced and yet, despite everything I endured, I was able to survive and consequently use the experiences for good. Some of the stories have been written through a filter while others have kept nothing back. They are all true. However, I do accept that minor details and dates might be questionable, and my mother's account of the incidents would differ from mine. I acknowledge there are always two sides to a story; here is mine.

My Family Background

- Eldest of four children, with the same father on our birth certificates. He later denied being our biological father.
- Father worked as an HGV driver during the day and as a barman five nights a week in a local public house.
- My father often came home at night drunk.
- Money was an issue and debt collectors would call at the house.
- Both my parents used physical violence on each other and also on my younger brother and sister and me.
- I had kind maternal grandparents who would buy us food, clothes and shoes.
- My parents divorced when I was twelve, on the grounds of adultery.
- My father had three wives and my mother had three husbands and one common law husband.
- My younger sister and youngest brother were treated different to my other brother and me.
- I was sexually abused by an uncle from the age of seven to ten. I told my mother but never told my father.
- My mother reacted by calling me a dirty bitch and saying that I had blackmailed my uncle.
- I lived with the guilt and the shame until the 19th of September 2012 when I told my mother I was not a dirty bitch and that I was a child with a mother who didn't care.
- My father died suddenly on my birthday in 1996 at the age of 74.

My Father

My father was the eldest of three brothers. I believe one brother lived in the next town, but I never met him. The younger brother was a successful businessman who lived in Wolverhampton with his wife and three children. I never knew my paternal grandmother as she had died of cancer before I was born. My grandfather lived in the same town when I was young but moved south. He was married three times and ran a Punch and Judy show on Brighton beach. I probably only met my grandfather three times.

My father had attended grammar school. I don't know what he did when he left school, as my only recollection when we lived together was that he was an HGV driver for a scrap metal company. I know prior to marrying my mother he was in the military police and spent time in India. (He would never eat dates as he said that amputees in India would pack the dates into boxes with their feet!).

He had been engaged to a girl who had died of TB before he married my mother. He wore his military uniform on their wedding day.

As well as working during the day he worked in the evening as a barman in a local public house. He played darts and snooker. I was told he had a good voice and used to sing in clubs, but I never heard him sing. He would often come home drunk, unfortunately alcohol had an adverse effect on him. There would be arguments and fights often resulting in me becoming involved, as my mother would shout for me to come downstairs. Whilst my father never expressed any affection towards any of us, he would sometimes pick me up and place me on his knee and brush my long hair. My mother would go to bed, and I would stay on his knee until he fell asleep, before I returned to my bed.

However, I did receive several beatings from my father when I was young. Looking back, it wasn't that he had witnessed anything I had done that deserved it. Rather it was when he came in from work and my mother told him that I had misbehaved. He would use a leather strap on my buttocks. One time the strap caught my face, which resulted in bruising, preventing me from going to school for several days. Having said that I felt I was favoured compared to my brother. My father would call me *Poppet*—a name I treasured when I was young.

When my father was home which wasn't often, as he went out every night except Monday and Wednesday when my mother went out, bedtime was always straight after Coronation Street had been on television. No negotiation, his word was law, and I would never dare to question anything he said or did. I never remember hearing him laugh when I was young—he always appeared to be angry and argumentative.

I was eleven when we left my father and moved to the next town. From that time, I saw him only twice. He took my brother and me out one Saturday afternoon was when I walked the six miles to his house. This was because I was so unhappy living with my mother and stepfather that I wanted to return and live with him. Unfortunately, he did not appear to be pleased to see me. He brought me straight back to my mother's house in his car and dropped me off at the door, as he told me he was going out. I never told him the reason why I had come to visit him, and he never asked the reason why.

He was married three times, but I believe he had several affairs. It is also rumoured that we have another stepbrother who carries the same forename as my own brother. This can never be validated as my father died suddenly on my birthday in October 1996. Prior to his death there was little contact between us. Following the birth of my eldest daughter, I sent him a letter, addressing it to the public house where I knew he used to work. Several months later on Easter Monday he came to find me, along with his second wife. We had our house up for sale, when I opened the door, he asked if he could view the property. Once inside he started to cry and said, "Lynne you don't know who I am do you?"

Following the reunion, I did have contact with him and his second wife. He still lived in the same town. Where I was born. Our relationship was superficial; I would very occasionally call to see them with my daughter. His second wife appeared very caring, and they seemed to be happy together. I believe she was several years older than him. Unfortunately, she died years later but I only discovered this when I visited him prior to Christmas to take them a Christmas gift.

Contact was lost again for a time until I received a letter from him giving me a new address. He was now on his own living in a flat. He was very involved with the British Legion in the town. He married a third time and moved again.

It was during a visit to see him and his wife that he told me that he was not my biological father. An injury during the war had resulted in his impotence. It transpired that my biological father was a man who had been a work colleague of my mother. He even told me his name.

His third wife died very suddenly of a heart attack one Wednesday afternoon in front of him. He rang me before her body had been removed from the house. From that time my involvement with my father increased. I would phone him twice a week and visit at least once every two weeks. He attended our eldest daughter's eighteenth birthday party and came to visit us one Christmas. My regret to this day is that I never found the courage to ask him to explain why he had told me I was not his biological daughter even though his name is on my birth certificate.

My Mother

My mother was an only child. My grandma had become pregnant prior to marrying my grandad. My grandma moved from Yorkshire to Lancashire when they got married. She had one brother who lived in Keighley with his wife and three children. Grandad had both a brother and sister who lived locally. My mother shared very little of her childhood memories with me. She said that my grandma was very strict with her and was often critical of her. She added that she loved my grandad, and he would defend her if she were in trouble with my grandma. When my mother left school, she went to work in a textile factory. She was engaged to someone else prior to marrying my father but this was broken off weeks before the wedding.

My mother and father were married during the war whilst he was on leave from the military police. When we were living with my father my mother never worked. She had four children, two daughters and two sons. We all have the same father's name on our birth certificates however we now know my youngest brother is the son of her second husband. It has been rumoured by a friend's mother that my sister is also the daughter of my mother's second husband and that my other brother is the son of a merchant sea captain who she used to write to; he visited her on several occasions. Unfortunately, no one ever had the courage to confront her about our biological fathers. She did however tell my sister that my youngest brother was indeed our stepbrother.

My mother was creative and liked to knit and make fancy dress costumes. She used to read tealeaves, and once told me she had a Romany gypsy guide who sent her messages. I remember her once setting up the Ouija board and seeing the glass spinning out of control and smashing on to the floor.

She left my father when I was eleven and we went to live in the next town with a man she later married who I now believe was the father of my youngest brother. He had no children, he worked as a motor mechanic repairing buses. They were divorced after only two years. My youngest brother stayed with him, confirming that he was his son. She then met a man who came to live with us in a two bedroom, rented house. He originated from Scotland and had no children.

They were together 13 years before he died suddenly of a heart attack; they never married. She then married a man she met through a dating agency, who also had no children. By this time, we had all left home and had moved away. She moved into his bungalow but fell out with the neighbours. There were several moves before they moved again to live nearer to my brother in Cheshire, initially in a mobile home, but that did not work out. The next move was into a housing association property. Her now third husband died of kidney failure in hospital. She never visited him when he was dying as she said it would upset her. Her youngest child, my brother, died of oesophageal cancer and again she refused to visit him in the hospice.

It proves difficult to write the basic life profile pertaining to my mother. She was very unhappy probably suffering with depression. There were occasions when I was young when she would stay in bed all morning and as a consequence we could not go to school. She was always falling out with friends and neighbours. There were also financial problems. I remember debt collectors calling at the house and having to hide until they went away. Life was just one crisis after another.

She has been denied so much through being unable to empathise, through seeing everyone as a means of feeding her own selfish motives. Interestingly the four men that she either married or cohabited with never had any children of their own. I now realise that my mother probably has a personality disorder called Narcissism.

A Breakthrough

I attended a workshop in 2013 promoting a Hawaiian healing therapy called Ho'oponopno, which we will discuss in more detail in Part Four. It entailed working with the Inner Child. During the preceding discussion a delegate suggested that I researched Narcissistic Personality Disorder (NPD), as my mother's profile fitted the description. She too had a mother who displayed the same characteristics as my mother.

I had a vague awareness of the term but had never related it to my own mother, despite her exhibiting the classic signs. I searched the Internet and was literally blown away with what I read. It explained so much as to why I had endured such a lack of love and recognition of my needs. Many of the nine recognised traits associated with NPD related to my mother. I ordered several books on NPD, which inspired me and motivated me to finish and publish this book. For the first time I was able to accept that my mother would never become the mother of my dreams, I would never hear words of praise or encouragement from her however much I had tried to please her and make her love me. Nothing I did would ever be good enough. I saw my mother through a different light. I had gained not only more awareness; it gave this book an extended focus and changed my attitude towards my mother. The understanding of my mother's indifference towards me was a result of her personality and nothing that I could have done or not done as a child would have changed her feelings towards me. It also lifted some of the guilt and blame of the abuse that I carried for so long. I acknowledged to myself that it really was not my fault; I was not to blame. My mother possibly had a personality disorder, perceiving things differently, which made her incapable of carrying out her role as a mother. If she had been a schizophrenic her behaviour would have been recognised and she would have received help and possibly therapy. NPD is not easily recognised and the person themselves cannot see there is a problem. It is everyone else who has the problem not them, which is a characteristic of the disorder. They too are victims, that has robbed them of so much.

Narcissistic Personality Disorder

Narcissistic Personality Disorder is a disorder in which a person has an inflated sense of self-importance as well as an intense preoccupation with themselves.

There are many definitions of NPD. Generally, they all identify the same characteristics.

The term Narcissism comes from Greek mythology and the story of Narcissus. He was very handsome, self- involved, and in love with his own image. He couldn't tear himself away from his reflection in a pool of water to become involved with anyone else. He died gazing at himself in the water.

The Diagnostic and Statistical Manual of Mental Disorders describes NPD as a personality disorder classified by nine traits.

- Has a grandiose sense of self-importance, e.g., exaggerates achievements and talents, expects to be recognised as superior without commensurate achievements.
- Is pre-occupied with fantasies of unlimited success, power, brilliance, beauty or ideal love.
- Believes that he or she is special and unique and can only be understood by or should associate with, other special or high- status people or institutions.
- Requires excessive admiration.
- Has a sense of entitlement i.e. unreasonable expectations of especially favourable treatment or automatic compliance with his or her expectations.
- Is interpersonally exploitative i.e., takes advantage of others to achieve his or her own needs.
- Lacks sympathy, is unwilling to recognise or identify with the feelings and needs of others.
- Is often envious of others or believes that others are envious of her.
- Shows arrogance, haughty behaviour or attitudes.

The above traits are demonstrated through behaviour, which focuses on their importance and their needs. Everything has to revolve around them. They lack empathy and are unable to show love to others.

Narcissistic mothers do not have children for the same reasons as others do. To a narcissistic mother the purpose of children is to have more mirrors of themselves. They expect their children to love them unconditionally, not the other way round. They have children to reflect their false image. They have children to abuse and control.

They do not see their role as a mother as life's biggest gift. It is a burden they did not expect. They thought they were creating little ME's. They do not realise that from the age of two, children start to develop their own personality and wills. This is unacceptable in a narcissistic mother's mind, resulting in her resenting her offspring and seeing them as spiteful and ungrateful little creatures. This is contra to aspirations of mothers whose greatest pleasure is to watch their children grow in independence and confidence. For the narcissistic mother this is viewed as an act of absolute betrayal.

Children express their emotions quite freely, which is a great annoyance to the narcissistic mother, as they cannot handle emotions. They end up resenting all the work that goes into raising a child unless they are reflecting their own image. Children are a nuisance to them taking precious time away from their own agendas. They do not like to shop for children's clothes, prepare meals, do their laundry, pay for things like dancing lessons, after school activities, school trips, organise birthday parties or buy gifts for the child.

There are two types of narcissistic parents—engulfing parents and ignoring parents.

Engulfing Parents

Children are seen as an extension of themselves not as an individual person. The child may have to care for their parents or siblings as a surrogate parent. This reduces the child's ability to relate to normal childhood. The parent will use brainwashing techniques to ensure the child keeps young and dependent on the parent. The engulfing parent will ignore all boundaries seeing no problem with reading emails and insisting that the child divulges personal information. The child is not allowed to have any interest that does not involve their parent.

Ignoring Parents

Children are viewed as separate to themselves. They can exhibit hostility towards the child and do not possess the caring, nurturing characteristics associated with good parenting. They have no interest in the child. In the extreme, parents can even ignore basic hygiene needs, or helping with schoolwork etc. The child is neglected and grows up feeling neglected and unloved, which can influence future relationships.

As I read through the characteristics of narcissism, I realised that it was so accurately describing my mother, and the consequence of my unhappy childhood. To a lesser degree I could also relate it to my father. These traits are evident when I recall my childhood memories. As you read about my childhood you will be able to recognise some of the traits that are exhibited through their individual behaviour. It may also give you, insight into your childhood experience as you recall your own childhood memories.

Home Alone

My parents were ignoring parents. My father appeared distant and was not involved in family matters or the lives of any of his children. This made my mother the main care provider. They were both physically abusive, as previously mentioned. My father was especially violent towards my brother. My mother showed no interest in the home. Clothes and bedding were seldom washed. The majority of my clothes were hand-me-downs from my grandma's brother's family who lived in Keighley. Food was sparse and we often lived off white bread and packets of crisps. My mother seldom cooked whilst she lived with my father. I felt we were seen as a charity case, due to both our appearance, and how we were often left to our own devices. There were other hardships too, my younger sister and brother appeared to be treated differently to my other brother and me by my mother.

This was more evident when we moved in to live with my stepfather. He not only favoured my younger siblings, he was very hostile towards me. My mother did nothing to protect me in fact she would find fault with me. I felt I could do nothing right. She would explode at me and lash out, kicking and punching. When my stepfather came in from work, she would tell him what I had done or what I had not done. My mother continued to refer to me as a 'dirty bitch', or a 'lazy bitch'. I was always a 'bitch'.

Using the identified traits of someone suffering with NPD I now understand why she acted in the way she did towards others. She excelled when she was admired. She constantly needed recognition and when she did not receive it, she would become hostile and aggressive towards people she saw as a threat. In later years she was very critical of my in-laws and my friends when they did not feed her ego. She constantly fell out with neighbours and had very few friends.

Both at my wedding and my eldest daughter's christening my mother caused a big scene. She started shouting in the bar area at my wedding because she was not given a drink before other guests. When I tried to calm her down, she shouted "it's because of all these bloody Christians at the bar that I didn't get a drink." She then stormed off refusing to greet guests as they entered the dining room.

At my daughter's christening, as parents, we promised to bring our daughter up in an alcohol, smoke, and drug free home. This caused my mother to hastily exit the church slamming the door behind her. When I approached her outside the church, she hurled abuse at me saying that due to the minister's comments and my promise, I was saying that she was not fit to be a grandmother. Her language was terrible and was heard by several people leaving the church.

Along with my grandma and my mother's common law husband they drove to our home and just sat in their car. I went out and begged her to come inside apologising for the way the minister had hurt her. Eventually she did come into the house, but the day had been ruined and caused a lot of unrest between my husband and his family. Once inside the house my mother demanded attention; I remember bringing her food and drinks as she sat refusing to engage in conversation with my in-laws and their family and friends. She later accused me and my husband's family of ignoring her, and for not taking photographs of her with our daughter. My mother could not see that she was the one responsible for causing friction and spoiling what should have been a lovely family occasion.

When my mother could no longer physically attack me, (which was still her pattern until I left home to get married), she continued to use verbal abuse, was never able to offer encouraging words and I can never recall her giving me any praise.

Returning to my childhood, my mother never attended parents evening at school. She never appeared interested in school reports and there were never any resources to buy books to help with my studies. At secondary school I often had to miss school when it was domestic science as my mother would not buy the ingredients to enable me to cook in the class. I never experienced the pleasure of creating anything and receiving positive feedback from her. This could be the reason why I tried so hard at school especially in exams in an attempt to gain praise and encouragement from the teachers.

Over the years my mother has said many cruel and unkind

66

things to me accusing me of many things that were not true. My mother's words included lies relating to my siblings She constantly told lies about each of us, resulting in fallouts and long periods of no communication amongst my siblings. My mother would often tell me that she had sacrificed her life for me, "I could have been happily married and had lots of money, but I left him because of you" (referring to when she left my stepfather). "I could have been a model and earned lots of money, but children ruined my figure"

My mother is the most unhappy person you would wish to meet; she has no empathy with anyone, and she is always right, she is jealous of people who she sees as superior to her. My mother is always the victim. I now know that she is a victim of herself because of her narcissism.

> *The way ahead is clear and free. I give myself permission to move out of the past with gratitude, and into a joyous new day*—Louise Hay

Several years ago, I was given a book, which was a catalyst for change in my life. It reinforced the fact that the love and approval that I had been desperately seeking from my mother was never going to happen. The book, written by two American psychologists, was called The Blessing. It explained how it is innate for us to seek our parent's blessings especially throughout our childhood. To be denied this birth right, results in spending our lives searching for love and acceptance. The essence of the book is to encourage the reader to accept that the blessing that they are desperately seeking is never going to happen. The book highlights the need to move on and obtain the denied blessing from other sources.

From reading the book, (which I have done several times, especially when I needed some verification and support.) I was able to accept that I could never change the course of my childhood and I could physically do nothing to replace the longing for a caring mother, it was in the past. The book challenged me to move on and seek the denied blessings in other forms. It also demonstrated that if I was to move on, I had to firstly forgive my mother We will explore the need to forgive in Part Four when we explore recovery and healing tools.

I Am NOT A Dirty Bitch

As you may recall in September 2012 my mother slammed the phone down on me. This was something she had done in the past, which had resulted in months of no contact. She had called me a dirty bitch again, a name I had grown up with. It was the words "dirty bitch" that hurt so much as it brought back all the painful memories of the sexual abuse I had suffered in my childhood.

On that day in 2012 something snapped inside of me. I screamed back "You have no right to call me that, I am not a dirty bitch. I was seven when it started, only a child, you should have protected me and stopped it." I had dared to retaliate which she could not accept so she slammed the phone down. Was it due to guilt or surprise that I had dared to speak up against her? I will never know as that day I decided that I would never allow her to hurt me again. I accepted that I was not that dirty bitch. I was a wounded child who had a sick mother.

Walking away from my mother reinforced a belief, that I had failed her. In my childhood I had been told that I should love and honour my parents. But there came a point when I could not take any more, like an alcoholic or someone who is dependent on drugs. I hit my rock bottom and the only way I could deal with my mother was to completely detach from her and start to focus on my own neglected needs, which involved working with my Inner Child, which is discussed in

Part Three.

Earlier I wrote a brief timeline of my mother's history. However, due to its factual content it does not allow you to see my mother in her true light. Whilst the following took place when I visited my mother before September 2012. I have tried to anticipate the reactions of a neutral observer, thoughts of the meeting.

There was an old lady who lived for herself

If you were able to look at my mother now you would see an old lady living alone with a little Yorkshire terrier dog as her closest companion. She would look deep into your soul and say "Look at me, my family do not care, no one cares. I have done everything for them, and this is how they repay me". You may feel disgust at her family, and wonder why has this poor old lady is being neglected by those who should be caring for her?

Your thoughts are disturbed by a knock at the door. A lady enters, the little dog is so pleased to see her, and starts to bark and chase around the room. The little old lady screams at the dog to shut up. The neighbour strokes the dog and attaches a lead to the dog's collar. Before she leaves to take the dog for a walk, she enquires how the old lady is feeling today asking about her painful knee and enquiring what she had eaten for lunch. "I just had some toast and a banana" she replies. "I thought your cleaner brought you lunch on a Monday when she came to do your cleaning?", the dog walker responds. "She doesn't clean anymore" the old lady replies. "I had to stop her; she charged me £10.00 and missed more than what she touched. She wasn't reliable bringing my dinner. I am a diabetic and needed to know when she was coming. One day it was after 1.30pm when she came as her car had broken down, they have two cars. Another time her son had an asthma attack and he ended up in hospital. Her husband did

69

not bring it until after 2.30pm." The lady and the dog leave.

The old lady looks at you and says, "I have only one son now who cares about me, but his wife does not like him coming here. I cannot stand her mother she thinks she is someone. I have two daughters, one occasionally rings but she always rings when the soaps are on the television. I know she works full time and has the children, but they are growing up now. She does visit me once in a while, but she says it is a long journey and weekends are busy. I bet she can find time to go out walking with her friends at weekends, but she cannot find time for me".

"I do not have anything to do with my other daughter, she is a wrong one has been all her life caused me so much trouble even when she was little. She broke up my marriage to my second husband. She was so ungrateful we moved to a lovely house in a different town to get away from my first husband who was a violent man. I should never have married him.

"I moved to Chester with my third husband he used to own a pet shop, he never had any children. We sold his bungalow, as I did not like the neighbours. I wanted to move nearer to my son who had moved to the Chester area when he got married, as his wife wanted to be near her mother. We bought a mobile home, but it was too cold in winter, so we put our name down for sheltered housing. We had to wait four years to get this house. Other people got a house in two years. My husband never liked it here. He used to spend hours in the back room either painting or photography—he spent a fortune on cameras. We used to go somewhere most days in the car. It was great to get out instead of staring at these four walls. But he died two years ago. Something wrong with his kidneys they said. I did not visit him in hospital as it was too upsetting for me. Anyway, with the cost of a taxi and to go on the bus meant changing in Chester was too much. My son took me a couple of times, but I had to give him the petrol money and pay the car park ticket".

"What about your daughters could they not have helped?" you may ask. "I was not speaking to the oldest one at the time she had given me a lot of abuse on the telephone and then slammed the phone down on me. The other one took me once."

Whilst you feel sorry for this little old lady you are aware that she has not said one positive thing about anything whilst you have been with her. But could you blame her for being so negative? You have an idea, I will come and visit you again next week, is there anything I could bring you is there anything you need? No, but it will be good to see you again she smiles. "I would offer you a drink, but the milk is not fresh. I had to cancel the milk man, he said I owed him two weeks and I know I had paid him the week before". As you leave, she takes your hand and says, "Thank you". You have an overwhelming desire to help this old lady but something deep inside does not feel right as you question how her children have deserted her in her hour of need. What you do not realise at that point is that you could easily become another person who will try and help her until she reveals her true character and takes advantage of your kindness, offering nothing in return but negativity and criticism.

I truly feel sorry for this old woman who is my biological mother who could never experience the joy and blessings children bring into your life as my own two lovely daughters have done, along with my precious grandchildren. She is hurting but I cannot help her. I almost believe that nothing can be done to rescue her from her misery, as in her mind she is always a victim of abuse of everyone who tries to help her.

As I am writing these words, I realise that despite my attempts to truly detach from my mother I am still emotionally connected to her. I resolve this by praying for her daily and asking for protection from any negative thoughts that she may direct towards me. A song, which has been very healing for me is from the Disney movie Frozen. The music is addictive, and the words are very powerful. I have slightly changed the lyrics below from a generic stance to one targeted to my own mother.

Let her go

The wind is howling like this swirling storm inside
Couldn't keep it in Heaven knows I have tried.
Don't let her in don't let her see
Be the good girl you always have to be
Conceal don't feel don't let her know
Well now she knows
Let her go, let her go
Can't hold it back anymore
Let her go let her go
Turn away and slam the door
I don't care what she is going to say
Let the storm rage on
She never really loved me anyway.
It's funny how some distance makes everything seem small
And the fears that once controlled me
Can't get to me at all
It's time to see what I can do
To test the limits and break through
No right no wrong, no rules for me
I am free

I am never going back; the past is in the past

My decision to divorce my mother has not been easy. Through my sister I learnt that once she tried to ring me but could not get through. Years ago, I would have acted on that and rung her back. Not because I relished the thought of re-establishing contact with her, it was the guilt of not being an obedient daughter who would not care for her own mother. It also had implications for my younger sister. As my mother advanced in years my sister became more involved with her despite living many miles away. This created tension and distance between my sister and me. My sister initially could not identify with my decision to completely detach from my mother, which I can totally understand. You need to walk in someone's shoes before you can really understand why people act the way they do.

Before I share with you, individual stories of my life I wanted to set the scene so to speak and give you a little background to my upbringing and how life events interweave. The purpose is to reach out to you. As part of my own healing therapy, I came to the conclusion that negatives can be turned to positives. This enabled me to accept that the bad things I encountered cannot be changed. It is how we deal with them that is important. I have tried to learn from the past and be able to use my experience to help others to move on like I have been able to do.

I came across this statement, which has enabled me to continue writing this book, especially when I was doubting myself and questioning my authority and capability to succeed and have the book printed.

"In a futile attempt to ease our past, we deprive the community of our healing gift. If we conceal our wounds and shame our inner darkness can neither be illuminated nor become a light for others"—Brennan Manning.

My Childhood Memories

There are many stories I could share with you regarding my relationship with my mother and the trauma of the sexual abuse. The ones I have selected to share with you took place when I was a child. As part of my healing journey, I needed to connect to my Inner Child. This involved revisiting my childhood and then writing about what resurfaced, which I recorded in story format over the years.

These were a source of strength, helping me to deal with the emotional issues that emerged. More importantly these stories enabled me to identify and connect with my Inner Child. A memory would emerge, and I would return to that place and the event would unfold. I was not there as a spectator I was there with all my senses. The pain would emerge, and it could be hours later before it went away, long after the story had run its course. Due to the stories being written over many years they vary in style. Several are written in the present tense, taken from my journals, whilst some are written in the past tense.

Bad Hair Day

One of my earliest memories, was when my mother, in a rage, cut off my long hair, which I used to wear in plaits. I must have been about five or six at the time as I remember going to school the following day and being asked why I had my hair cut. My mother told my grandma and neighbours that I had cut my own hair. As I previously explained one thing my father used to do when he was at home was to brush my hair. I loved it; I felt special. He would sit in his chair, and I would sit on his knee, and he would brush my long hair getting rid of the all the knots and tangles. Being close to him was very special.

After the incident my father never brushed my hair again

even when my hair grew. I think my mother's motive was two-fold—to spite my father, but also to punish me, she was jealous of my father's attention toward me.

Another issue was the lies she told, about not allowing anyone to brush the knots out of my hair, telling my grandma that when she had threatened to brush out the knots in my hair, I had cut my hair. Yet that was exactly what my father was doing gently untangling my knotted hair.

As a child I witnessed my mother telling lies on many occasions. It was as if she not only distorted the truth, she convinced herself that what she said was true. I cannot recall in any depth the feelings the incident provoked other than to say I hated my short hair and to this day I have never had my hair cut short, which I believe is attributed to the negative feelings associated with the incident.

Go away

The door opens slowly with little noise, through closed eyes and clenched teeth I experience the infusion of light into the room. I will every muscle in my body to be still as I try to breathe as in sleep, I am conscious of my erratic breathing so slowly I turn on to my side with my face into the pillow. My heart is pounding along with my head, which is listening to my heart as it sings 'Please go away, please go away, please go away', each time getting louder in my head 'Please go away, please go away'.

He stays at the door I sense his intention

I lie there waiting for him to speak my name, and then pull the bed covers back.

I listen for my name I wait for contact. Nothing

Too scared to open my eyes I listen intensely then I

75

hear the closing of the door. Then silence. The only noise I hear is my own heart pounding as it rocks within my rib cage trying to escape.

Slowly I open my eyes just in case he's still there then I wait.

Nothing

I then slowly turn over. I realise that I am crying silent tears but no sound.

I turn my head; he has gone. My body erupts in spasm as I start to shake followed by a deep cry. I put my finger in my mouth and bite it to stop the noise I am making.

I am safe now she will be home soon before my father gets home

I am hurting, I am remembering.

I am a child who had no one to protect me.

I have a mother who doesn't love me.

Each time I read this memory it is still painful but not as intense as in the past, which I feel demonstrates my own healing.

Rain, rain, go away come back another day, but never on a Friday

It is raining so hard that it is bouncing off the toilet block roof. The sky is black, the day is black, it is not going to stop raining so I won't be able to play out tonight. It hurts, not a like a slap that stings then goes away. This hurt never goes away, it will even hurt tomorrow and make that a black day too.

Due to the rain we have to sit quietly in the hall at playtime. I am glad we have to sit quiet; I do not want to talk or play, I feel sick. I start to cry and put my hand to go to the toilet. Mr Bury asked me why I was crying I told him my goldfish had died. It was not a real lie as Anita had died a few weeks ago. I had won her at the fairground, but my mother would not let me keep her, so I had given the fish to my grandad. I chose the name Anita. It was a special name that I used to call myself. I would imagine that I lived with one of my mother's friends who I called auntie, who was very kind to me she could even make me feel better on a Black Saturday. I never told her about what used to happen on a Friday night, I was frightened she would not love me anymore.

Mr Bury gave me a disbelieving look and he told me to go to the toilet and blow my nose. But no one believes me when I tell the truth. You see my father does not know my mother goes out every Friday night once he has gone to the pub and my uncle babysits. My mother goes out Monday and Wednesdays and my father goes out Tuesdays, Thursdays, Fridays, Saturdays and Sundays. They never stay in together, we never do anything, as a family, the only time we are all together for anything is Sunday morning when my dad cooks Sunday dinner. For me it is the best time ever but not for my brother. He is not very good at holding a knife and fork and dad stares at him, which makes him worse. Dad will then shout at him, telling him he eats likes a dog and to get away from the table. My brother is not allowed to finish his meal.

When this happens, I know my mother will start to find fault with me. She will watch me, waiting for me to mess up and then she can lash out either physically or verbally at me. I know she loves the others more than me especially my brother. When she is in a bad mood, she always takes it out on me.

My mother says that whilst everyone likes me, they do not really know how bad I am inside. She says that they spoil me and not my brother. That is not true as even though my auntie and uncle are not rich, they buy us both comics and sweets every Friday. I always go there for my tea on a Friday. My auntie is my grandad's sister. She is very kind; we go for long walks in the summer and take picnics with us. She is so thin that once she got her leg stuck down a cattle grid, which was very scary. My uncle is not nice like my auntie. He makes rude signs at people and wears white pumps. He told me there was no Father Christmas, which made me cry. But he did not care, he never cares when I cry.

One time I told my auntie what he was doing, she became angry and said it was not true and that I should not tell anyone as I would be stopped from coming to their house on a Friday. She said my uncle loved me and I was his daughter that he never had. I remember her saying that he would never hurt me and when I said that he did hurt me, she said that if I told anymore lies, she would wash my mouth out with soap and water. I knew she was not joking as she had once washed my brother's mouth out, when, he swore at my mother.

Another incident that came to me whilst working with my Inner Child and involved the sexual abuse is best described in story mode.

Let there be light but not tonight

The pain in my tummy is getting worse. I need to go to the toilet but where can I go? It is so dark now and I should be inside, but he will be waiting for me. Mum will not be home for at least another hour as it is only 9.00pm according to our neighbour's kitchen clock. I always crouch down in the small passageway between their house and our house. It leads to the garden and the back door. It is dark there and no one can see you. I do not like having to urinate there, but I do not like what might take place if I go inside to use the toilet. I hate the toilet; it is at the top of the stairs and the door makes a noise when you try and close it. It is like entering a dark cave with no escape.

Tonight, the kitchen light has been left on next door, it has been on since it went dark but there is no one in the kitchen. It is lighting up the passageway and you can see the passageway from the road. No one else is playing out now they have all been called in ages ago. Mr Shipley from across the road saw me a few minutes ago when he was taking Rusty his dog for a walk and told me he had seen my uncle looking for me and I needed to go home.

Maybe if I was very quiet, I could sneak in, use the toilet and come back out and wait until I saw my mum being dropped off at the top of the road. I could then go in the house and tell him my mum is on her way home. That sounded the best plan as I could not wait any longer—I really needed to go to the toilet.

I walked down the passageway, carefully I opened the back door. It made no noise; Beauty our dog was not in the washroom which was good as she would have come to me for hugs and kisses. The washroom door was open into the kitchen, the only sound was the TV in the front room and the glass door allowed light to shine on the bottom of the stairs. I very carefully walked towards the light plotting my path to avoid any obstacles. I could see the wheels of my sister's pram as the light reflected the silver trim as I passed the hall towards the front door and the stairs. Approaching the stairs, I almost retreated back the way I had come, as I knew that if he found me on the stairs my escape would be blocked.

I started my ascent slowly but halfway up the stairs fear overtook me. I needed to be as quick as possible because he may come looking for me again and see me or come upstairs and check on my brother and sister. Quickly trying not to make any sound I reached the toilet door, which was open. I cannot remember if I closed the toilet door completely or left it slightly open. But I do remember the door been pushed open and hearing him say, "I have been looking for you".

Doomsday Calling

In 1962 the Cuban missile crisis was dominating the Media; it was on the news and the front page on a newspaper. As a young child with limited understanding, it made me feel insecure and afraid. I was at this point being subjected to the sexual abuse of which I feel was instrumental in making me feel insecure and afraid.

The incident I recall involved my mother going out and leaving me alone in the house whilst she went out taking my siblings with her. I asked to come with them, and she refused. I told her I was scared that the end of the world was going to happen and begged her not to leave me alone. She was totally detached from my fear. I can remember crying and trying to get out of the house when she opened the front door. As they went down the road I stood there crying and screaming not to be left. I eventually returned to the house and went upstairs and got into bed under the covers, listening for the bombs to come and destroy the world. I can remember the smell of the dirty bed sheets. When I could not stand it anymore, I decided to get up and go outside, and wait. Once outside a neighbour saw me and asked me why I was crying and why I was not at school. I told her that I was scared as it was going to be the end of the world and that my mother had gone out and left me.

She invited me into her house and made me a drink and let me play with her pedigree pug dogs. Whilst I cannot remember what she said about the Cuban missile threat, just being with her made me feel safe. What a contrast from the emotions that I associated with my mother who constantly created fear through her physical and emotional abuse. When my mother returned, I went back home. Nothing was ever mentioned about the incident again.

My father too had a very sadistic streak. Talking to my brother recently together we recalled several traumatic incidents that we had both encountered before we left my father and went to live with our stepfather in the next town. (Writing 'stepfather' to describe my mother's second husband does not give an accurate description of him, as he was never a father to us).

I am amazed at how much we both can remember of those dark days when we were young. Traumatic experiences are imbedded in our cellular memories, which we will explore later.

Storm inside and outside

As you know my father was an HGV driver and very occasionally, he would take my brother and me to the docks on his early morning run. We both loved it. We would sit on the large warm engine in the cab. I remember it being very noisy. My father was rarely at home, he had both a day job and worked five nights a week as a barman in a local public house. He would often come home drunk, and the arguments would start. The drink made him aggressive, and he and my mother would physically fight and throw things at each other. Despite money always being an issue, we always had dogs. They were never fed adequately or went to visit a vet if they were ill. One time Beauty, our black and white crossbreed, had a sharp tin can attached to her mouth and we could not get it off. She was in great distress and had to wait until my father came home from work for him to release the can from her mouth. My father was not a dog lover and my brother, and I clearly remember a night following a fight with my mother, when he threw a puppy on the fire. Even now the trauma of that incident is still raw. I am also aware that all the other puppies just disappeared one day.

I had always been afraid of thunderstorms, during a storm my auntie would make me go under a table with her and remove any metal clips I had in my hair and then proceed to tell me stories of how thunderbolts could destroy homes by coming down the chimney and setting fire to the house. I was petrified and so was she. If it thundered whilst I was outdoors, I would panic and run inside for cover.

My parents were aware of my fear as one time I got a beating from my mother for running back from the shop when it started to thunder before I got the items of food she needed. Late one night there was a severe thunderstorm. My father had returned from the pub worse for drink. I have no idea what caused him to do this but he grabbed both my brother and me and literally throw us out into the garden and locked the door so we could not get back into the house. We were both petrified running aimlessly around the garden. I had been told not to seek shelter under a tree during a thunderstorm; the garden contained a large willow tree, which added to the terror. This was intensified by a frightening image of my father standing at the window laughing at us. Each time there was a flash of lightening it exposed his sadistic grin. We were left out until the storm subsided and eventually my mother let us in when he had gone to bed. In retrospect I realise that my father did not treat me any better than my mother. Whilst he was not as violent towards me as my mother, he never exhibited any love or emotional support.

Cinderella's Carriage

Another occasion when my mother lied involved her blaming me in front of the police for a vicious poem she had written to my father's girlfriend, which was seen as a threat to her life. My mother was so talented at writing stories and poems. I would have been about eleven as it was when my parents were getting divorced. She made me hand write the poem and address the envelope.

I can still remember the poem:

Cinderella, has you ride home in your coach of grey

with lover boy by your side to end a perfect day

as you sit there as a queen in the place where his wife

should have been.

enjoy your ride at 521 as very soon you will see it will be the

last you take in that certain VPP.

(My father owned a grey car, and the number plate was VPP 521).

The police gave me such a drilling, whilst my mother assured them that I would be punished. I never uttered a word in my defence, as I was too scared of my mother. To this day I find it hard to come to terms with not just that incident but also the many other cruel things she has inflicted on me, which was the thread throughout my childhood.

When my brother, sister and I have shared childhood memories, we have discovered that my mother has a totally different perspective on the things that we endured in our childhood. She is totally oblivious to that her behaviour caused so much hurt and grief.

The following stories are all related to the bullying I encountered. Although my parents were not directly involved in the bullying, I do believe that if they had been more supportive and responsible parents many of the incidents could have been avoided.

Get it off

One traumatic experience, which still evokes feelings of pain, and rejection, involved being bullied over a period of time at primary school by a group of four girls in my class. They would walk behind my brother and me on the way to school and call me names and physically push me and grab my school bag and throw it into the road. I never told anyone what they did, or the cruel names they called me. Whilst it was no secret what they were doing it was just something else that I carried deep within, which reinforced my belief that I was not a nice person and that there was something wrong with me.

The bullying initially involved a special friend; my mother and her mother knew each other from their school days. Previous to the bullying I would stay at her house overnight during the holidays. We were good friends and we both wanted to be nurses when we grew up. I discovered later that we did both become nurses. She was able to go straight from education into nursing, but I had to wait and enter the profession as a mature student in my early thirties.

She had a secret; she suffered with enuresis, on more than one occasion I woke up in the night with my nightdress and hair wet. Her mother would run a bath and wash my hair and nightclothes before I went home. My friend would cry and get upset. It was never discussed, I never told anyone about her secret. I was good at keeping secrets. I just accepted it, I loved to stay at her house. Another thing I liked was that her mother would give me clothes that were too small for my friend. One reason could have been due to the fact that my clothes were generally hand me downs that usually did not fit me properly or in need of a wash and certainly they were never colour coordinated. I remember clearly her mother giving me two dresses to take home. She wrote a note asking for some money for the dresses. Unfortunately, my mother refused to pay for them. The problem for me was she did not return the two dresses and instead she made me wear them. Things changed between my friend and me when she stopped wetting the bed. She had been given a special buzzer that woke her up if any moisture went on a special pad. Over a period of time, she started playing with other girls and leaving me out, to the point where she became one of the four girls who used to bully me constantly at school. Her new best friend lived nearer to her house and so they started to walk to school together and spend time together after school. Previously when it came to sports my friend and I were always the last two to be chosen to be in a team of rounders or netball, we would then end up in the opposing teams. I hated netball and rounders, I would either drop the ball if it was passed to me, or I would be constantly apologising if I ran into someone. I also hated taking off my clothes, as I never had the correct PE equipment, which meant I had to wear just a top and my knickers. But now my special friend was getting better at playing netball and rounders, as I watched them practising at playtimes.

On the day of the bullying incident, I pleaded with my mother not to make me wear one of the dresses for school. I tried to explain that my friend had told some of the girls in my class that the dresses used to be hers and that I had not paid for them. My mother was unconcerned and became even more determined that I would wear the dress. I had no option but to go to school in the dress. I never dared to argue with my mother, one wrong look would result in a beating or at least a crack across the head. When I arrived at school, they were all waiting for me by the gate. They recognised the dress and told me to take it off or to pay the money I owed. Thankfully once in class and at the following playtime they did not pursue me, and I was able to keep out of their way.

However, I was not as fortunate after lunch. In the playground they all ran towards me shouting "GET IT OFF, GET IT OFF". For a second, I just froze and then I started to run to the toilet block to escape their taunting words. I had remembered which toilet doors locked or my ordeal could have been much worse, if they had been able to physically attack me. Standing there inside the locked toilet with my heart pounding I looked down at the dress. It did not even fit me; the sleeves were too long and had to be turned back. I hated the dress and my mother for making me wear it.

"Get it off, get it off"; they screamed as they banged and kicked the door. One of the girls tried to climb over by standing on the toilet next door. The others were trying to push her over the top of the cubicle. After several failed attempts I could hear them planning what to do next. They started throwing small pebble stones off the walls of the toilet block. They then found larger stones to throw into the toilet cubicle. One of the stone did hit me on the head. But that was nothing compared to what I heard them discussing. Their plan was to wait until home time, and once away from school they would rip the dress off me. They discussed it in detail where the attack would take place. Even how far I would need to walk home in my vest and knickers. I heard them mention my coat. They agreed to take that too and then hide it where I would not be able to find it.

I heard the bell ring to end playtime, following a barrage of threats they left and returned to class. Once they had gone the emotion took over and I started to cry. I was so scared so frightened. I felt physically sick. Trembling I knelt down over the toilet and stuck my fingers down my throat to make myself sick, making sure that the vomit went down the front of the dress. After wiping my eyes and blowing my nose I unlocked the toilet door and slowly walked to towards school hoping that my plan would get me out of this ordeal.

I was met by Mr Watts, the school caretaker. He was a kind man and knew everyone's first name. Observing my red eyes and stained dress, he told me to sit down. He went to get my teacher who asked me if there would be anyone home to look after me? I said yes not knowing or caring if I would go home to a locked door. My only concern was to escape the planned attack that was to follow if I stayed at school.

When I got home my mother was home, observing the dress she told me to take it off and put it into the bin. My mother did not wash our clothes often, I guess she did not like the idea of a soiled dress being left in the wash house sink. This actually gave me another idea regarding the other dress that had not been paid for. A few days later I wore it to play out and deliberately ripped the bodice from the skirt making a large hole in the bodice. I told my mother I had got the dress stuck on some barbed wire as I had tried to get free. I honestly cannot remember if I received a crack from her on that occasion but if I did, it was nothing compared to what might have happened if she had made me wear the dresses again for school.

Another incident of bullying I clearly remember at school, involved a physical fight. I cannot remember what the issue was about. I just seemed to be someone that got picked on amongst my peers. I was quiet, withdrawn and did everything I could to avoid conflict. There was so much conflict in the home setting with my parent's constant fighting and arguing. I would do anything to avoid confrontation.

I can remember the fight took place in the schoolyard. I was knocked to the ground and dragged along by my hair, which was in a long plait. I can to this day remember what I was wearing. I had green and white checked tights a purple coat. Most of the others wore grey uniforms. So again, I was different and an easy target. I ended up with grazed knees and elbows, a hole in the coat through being dragged along. A teacher had observed the event and made the girl apologise to me the following day. (Thankfully today the incident would have been investigated further and appropriate action taken).

The Christmas tree with no needles

The bullying continued but not always in a physical way. They would often take exercise books and pencils from my desk and hide them. One time my needlework went missing during a lesson, it was of a Christmas tree. I had gone to get a different colour of thread and when I returned to my desk the needlework had disappeared. I knew they had hidden it due to their smirks and giggles. Mrs Smith was the strictest teacher in school so to lose my needlework would result in punishment. I went to tell her that it had disappeared expecting the worse. To my amazement she stood up and told the class that they had better find my needlework or they would stay in every playtime until it was found. We then both went outside. I started to cry, she said nothing but put her hand on my shoulder and gave me a nice smile. It was something very special. I craved affection and to be loved. This kind gesture was so meaningful to me.

When we went back into class my needlework was on my desk. I later discovered from another classmate that it had been hidden behind a radiator. Mrs Smith was always nice to me after that incident. I think she along with other teachers knew I was being bullied at school. Bullying in the 60s was just seen as part of growing up and was overlooked just like child sexual abuse. People knew it was going on but did nothing to stop it.

Showcase for bullying

The bullying continued in secondary school, it did not involve the same girls as they, apart from my special friend, had all gone to a different school in the same town. My former friend did not want to associate with me, so I found myself alone again. There are two significant occasions, which I can recall, where my mother was instrumental in me becoming a target for bullying causing ridicule amongst my peers at school.

Whilst it did not result in physical bullying, it involved verbal taunting, reinforcing my self-hate and self-disgust. It was traumatic and resulted in me feeling alone and unloved.

It involved the local carnival and being made to compete in the fancy-dress competition. In the past she had made me, and my siblings take part in the fancy-dress completion when we lived with my father. I had once been a gypsy wearing a scarf around my head with all coins draped on it, a Hawaiian dancer with a grass skirt, and a belly dancer. My mother was very good at making the costumes and on more than one occasion one of us would win a prize. Once the judging had taken place you joined the carnival procession and walked through the town displaying your certificate if you were fortunate to win one. When I was younger, I did not find the event stressful. But at thirteen the whole process filled me with dread. So much so that I actually told my mother I did not want to do it. As always this made her even more determined that she would have her way, with no negotiation. I was made to dress up as an Indian squaw. I wore a short sack with beads sewn all over it. My long hair was in plaits with a band and a feather around my head. Even now the image haunts me. I was so embarrassed. To make matters worse I did not win a prize. My mother blamed me and said that I had not smiled at the judges and had looked away when they had approached me. The consequence was that I had been seen by my peers and had to take a lot of ridicule from that at school. Even older girls taunted me on the corridor and at play times.

Another event similar to the fancy-dress competition, involved being made to enter a beauty competition for the Carnival Princess. I would again have been twelve or thirteen. The memories are vivid. It entailed the contestants parading round a room in front of the judges. They then selected six of us to go forward to the next round. There were two parts to this round, walking around the hall on your own and then being interviewed by the judges using a microphone. What an ordeal. I was shy and self-conscious, and although I managed to walk around the room the interview was a disaster. I mumbled avoided eye contact and made a real fool of myself. Consequently, I came fifth out of the six. This resulted in my mother's wrath and walking home she challenged me. I had kept my head to one side, which was something I do even now if I find myself in a vulnerable position, my head automatically gravitates to the right. The more I tried to verbally defend myself the more annoyed she became with me.

At school on the Monday once again I was the source of ridicule. The winner of the Carnival Princess was the sister of a girl in my class, she her comments were not kind. I remember being told by one girl, that my face looked like a cow's backside. Another said I had worn false boobs for the competition. There were other comments all of which made me even more withdrawn and unhappy. If only I had someone, I could have shared the pain with. But experience demonstrated that to share from the heart can have traumatic consequences.

New Town, New Home, New School, New Dad

My mother had left my father in the June before I had officially left junior school. This resulted in us moving to the next town to live with a man who she eventually married. This was the man that she had been seeing secretively on a Friday night, during which time the sexual abuse had taken place. I remember walking home from school one day with my brother and seeing a grey van parked in front of our house. I was told to get into the van as we were leaving my father and going to live in the next town. I was not allowed to go into the house. My younger brother and sister were already in the van, along with a few of their toys and two suitcases containing some clothes. The whole of the summer holidays was traumatic living with "Uncle Bill" that is what we were told to call him.

We were imprisoned in a house, as not allowed out for fear of being seen by father, with no toys and nothing to do

It became obvious that my sister and younger brother already knew Uncle Bill. I discovered that they would go and see him with my mother during the day as he worked at a local garage part time and worked evenings repairing buses. He was very strict especially with my brother and me. Apparently in the war he had been a Captain's Batman, the house was run on military lines. Each evening we had to be inspected, he would look at our fingernails and behind our ears and necks to see if there were any tidemarks. We were made to go to bed early even at weekends. I had no toys or books and the few toys I possessed had been left behind. I hated this new living arrangement. I missed my father, grandma and grandad, so much as now I could not walk to their house. I felt trapped. But no one cared. My mother never tried to make the transition easier by offering support; she had no empathy and was unable to see the effect it was having on my brother and me. I now realise that this again was due her personality disorder.

It was within these first few weeks that my brother and I found some cards in one of their bedroom drawers. My mother and stepfather had gone shopping taking my younger brother and sister with them as they often did. They never took my other brother and me, which again reinforced the fact that we were not treated the same as my younger brother and sister. The cards we found were given over several years, valentine's cards, birthday cards, Christmas cards to each other. But the one card that blew me away was one that said, "Congratulation on the birth of our son". I realised that was why my younger brother and sister were treated differently to us. I wanted to tell my father what I had discovered. I was annoyed that my father had received all the blame and painted as a bad man. I felt a loyalty towards my father. After this revelation I started to dislike Uncle Bill even more.

For me this was a very unhappy time. The word "ostracised"

comes to mind. My mother continued with her abusive behaviour towards me. She appeared to constantly be on my case finding fault with me over the most tedious things. Her violent streak was still evident, she was unhappy and probably depressed but to my knowledge she never sought any medical intervention. She too had very few friends in the new town.

Hallelujah pass the biscuits

During this time my brother and I started going to church. It came about due to the church holding a street meeting near to our house and we were invited to attend Sunday school. In many ways this became a refuge for me. It was here I met some lovely, kind people. I became involved in lots of the activities, including Girl Guides, a singing group and bible study classes. For several years I obtained 100 per cent attendance at Sunday school, which was reflected in a book prize you received each year displaying your attendance.

Things were still very volatile at home; I was still unhappy. This resulted in me attention seeking at church. I went through a period of having nosebleeds. I remember on more than one occasion making my nosebleed to gain the attention of a lady who was a nurse. She would attend to me in such a loving, caring way. The fact that she put her arm around me and actually touched me in a therapeutic way was very significant. I realise now that as a child I was very much deprived of any meaningful touch. My mother was unable to cuddle and communicate in a physical way. Her physical contact was through lashing out. There were never any goodnight kisses when I went to bed. No night- time stories. Apart from schoolbooks and Christmas annuals there were never any books in the house. This could account for my passion for books today.

I promise on my honour to do my best

Whilst my mother never attended any of the church activities, she generally never stopped me from going as long as it did not cost her any money. She would never allow me to attend music school or guide camp or anything that involved money. But it was not always the money, that was the reason why she would not allow me to attend many of the activities.

My friends had gone to Guide camp in the Yorkshire Dales. A lady and her husband who were the grandma and grandad of one of my friends took me with them to the open day. Unfortunately, one of the guides had become unwell and her parents decided to take her home. The guide leader asked if I wanted to come and stay at the camp for the last two days. It was agreed that my friend's granddad would take me home and ask my mother if I could go and stay for the last two days. When I got back and asked her, she said 'no', telling my friend's grandad that I did not deserve to go. She told him how disrespectful I was to both her and my stepfather. No negotiation, despite him reassuring her that it would not involve any money. I cried so much it hurt. Once he had gone, she said nothing but today I can still see that smirk on her face and her piercing eyes, I believed that she actually enjoyed punishing me in any form she could.

Honour your Father and Mother

Another occasion which is significant, and to some point accounts for why I have defended my mother throughout the years, involved my mother taking me to the minister's house. I would have been around thirteen at the time. There had been an argument with my stepfather, I cannot remember what I had done or said to him that caused him to tell me I was ungrateful, and he resented having to support me.

My mother had gone to the church, but the minister was not

there. She asked for his private address. When we arrived at his home, she told him what an unruly child I was, and that I was the cause of all the friction in the house. How my stepfather provided for me and ungrateful I was, explaining that my father had been a violent man towards her. She painted a very dark picture of my father, telling the Minister that she had to leave to protect us. However, she did not say that she was having an affair with my stepfather or how violent she was towards me. My mother started to cry. His wife made us all a drink. As always, I said nothing out of fear of what would happen later if I told the Minister how my stepfather treated me compared to my siblings.

The outcome was that I received a verbal telling off from the Minister. He said he was surprised at my behaviour towards my stepfather. He quoted scripture to me, telling me to read my Bible and to ask Jesus to help me to be good. He then said a prayer. This was very traumatic for me. The sense of belonging to the church had been shattered. I felt the Minister was saying it was my fault that my mother was unhappy, and that I was making things difficult for all the family. My mother was right—it was me. I was a bad child.

Despite the reprimand from the minister and me trying to please my stepfather nothing changed within the family unit, in fact things became worse for me. I can now see that the marriage was doomed. There were now lots of arguments between them over money, there was also a falling out with his sister who he was close to. My mother had taken a dislike to both his sister and her husband. She became annoyed if he went to visit his sister. My mother constantly had issues with other people which resulted in her having arguments with neighbours. It appeared she also had a dislike for anyone in authority. My brother was in hospital at the time with a brain tumour, which also added to the stress and friction within the house.

A time for sharing and caring

Two years after my mother and stepfather married things were not working out. It is not surprising when you consider the obstacles they had to overcome. Happy families do not come ready made. They require investing time, energy and love. That just did not happen. There was constant friction, which came to a dramatic end between Christmas and New Year. It involved my grandma and grandad coming over for a meal on Christmas Day. Grandad had come with me to take the dog a walk. He was such a kind man, and I missed my grandma and grandad so much as I could not just walk down the street to see them like I did when we lived with my father, as we now lived several miles away from them.

When we lived nearer, they would buy us children's clothes and shoes. I can remember my grandad saying "Mary, look at her shoes they are too small for her." They would take me on a bus to Manchester and buy both me and my brother clothes for birthday and Christmas. My younger brother and sister always appeared to have nicer clothes and lots of toys. (This was evident at Christmas as the younger ones always got more presents than my brother and me).

During our walk that night I shared with my grandad that I missed them so much and that I did not like my stepfather because of how he treated me. I told him that I was not allowed to be in the same room as my stepfather when he came in from work. That I had to be in bed before my younger brother went to bed. I was not allowed to have any meals with my stepfather. He would not talk to me. How he would buy everyone in the house ice creams from the van that came down the street and not get one for me. Even now typing those words brings back the feelings of rejection. I can see them all eating their ice cream. Any opportunity he had to vent his anger and frustration was targeted at me. He purposely would bang into me. But the thing that caused me the most hurt was the rejection I felt living there.

My grandad must have challenged my mother and stepfather once I had gone to bed. The following night I was in bed and heard them arguing again downstairs. The focus of the shouting involved me, and what I had told my grandad. They came into the bedroom. "I will show her whose house this is, if she doesn't like my rules, she can go and live with her grandad, see if he likes living with an ungrateful lazy bitch? Let her go and live with her wonderful dad who pays nothing to support her". He then tried to drag me out of bed, which made me scream out as I expected the worse. This resulted in my youngest brother crying in the next bedroom along with my sister in the bunk bed below.

It was difficult for him to reach me in the top bunk as I moved away from the edge and into the corner of the bed near the wall. Grabbing my foot he said, "You have ruined Christmas for this family, you cause nothing but trouble in this house. I never wanted you to come here, ask your mother. But I took you in. Whilst I truly cannot remember his exact words. I do remember my mother parting words. "I hope you will be satisfied when we are walking the streets tomorrow."

Lynne, don't leave me

The following morning my mother instructed me to take my little brother to my stepfather's sister. She had packed him a bag with some of his toys. My mother told me that my stepfather was going to throw me out and I could not live there anymore due to my behaviour towards him. I remember saying I would go and live with my grandma and grandad. Hurtfully she said that they did not want me, and that she was going to take me to Social Services.

My youngest brother and I were quite close. I was nine years older than him and would often adopt the mother role, taking care of some of his basic needs. I remember the walk with my little brother, being only three or four he was not yet at school. He was wearing a grey and blue coat, along with a little blue peaked cap. He had beautiful eyes, the colour of sapphires unlike me with my brown eyes. We held hands all the way. I cannot remember what we talked about. But I do remember his parting words to me as I handed him over to my stepfather's sister. His words have haunted me ever since. I had explained to him on the journey that I was going to leave and live somewhere else, as our stepfather had said I could not live there anymore. Once we arrived, I rang the doorbell. I think they were expecting my brother, as they did not ask me why I was bringing him. Neither did they ask me to go into the house. My brother would not go into the house. I tried to let go of his hand and move away. But he held my hand so tightly, which resulted in my stepfather's sister grabbing his other hand and pulling him away from me. Writing this all these years later the emotion it contained is still there. His last words to me were "Lynne don't leave me". I can still see his little face and his tears, one hand reaching out to me and his other hand firmly in the grip of his auntie.

I did not realise when I left my little brother that my mother was also leaving my stepfather and my little brother. At that point I thought she was just taking me to Social Services and my stepfather would pick up my brother once he returned from work and she had returned from Social Services.

The outcome was we did go to Social Services, but they would not intervene. My grandparents said they could not accommodate all of us. Waiting at the bus stop, with my mother, brother and sister we met a lady who was the mother of one of my friends from church. She was on her own with three children. She invited us to go and stay with her until my mother could find alternative accommodation.

I never saw my younger brother again until I was married with two children. I later discovered he had spent time living in Canada and had joined the forces. To my knowledge my mother had no contact with him, from the day I took him and left him with his auntie. He died of oesophageal cancer when he was only in his forties. Thankfully we had been reunited and both my sister and I were able to attend both his daughter's wedding and his funeral, which took place within four weeks of each other. My mother did not attend his funeral and refused to visit him in the hospice.

Hello, I am Bill

My mother, brother, sister and I eventually moved into rented accommodation, the house consisted of two bedrooms, an outside toilet and a bath and sink in the largest bedroom that I shared with my mother. My brother and sister slept together in a double bed, The house was dirty, my mother never cleaned, or washed clothes, bedding on a regular basis. I can never remember her washing any bedding whilst we lived there as we had no washing machine and clothes were washed by hand. Money was a big issue now. We would often be hungry, cream crackers and a drink of Oxo often constituted a meal. Many nights there was no money to feed the electric meter. I remember vividly how the three of us would sit on the Chapel of Rest wall, which was next door but one to our house under the streetlight, because it was too dark to do anything in the house. We would scare ourselves silly by talking about ghosts and dead bodies. My mother's violence continued; she would often smash things in the house and on more than occasion broke windows by throwing an object against it.

One Christmas morning I got up and came downstairs to find a man asleep on the settee, I woke him up when I put on the light. "Hello, my name is Bill" he said. Bill never left from that day. He was kept a secret from my grandparents for several weeks, we were warned not to tell them. Compared to my previous stepfather Bill was nice. He worked, so the financial burden was eased. He spoke to me and for the first time ever my mother appeared happy. He lavished her with gifts, and they would spend time together. He inherited grandad's car when he died.

Following Bill's arrival, I now had to share a bed with my siblings until they got my brother a single bed. Whilst it was not ideal as personal washing had to be done either in their bedroom or downstairs, things at this point were tolerable at home. However, one memory I have of that time involved Bill's mother and aunt coming down from Scotland to stay with us for a week. Due to the house only having two bedrooms they had to sleep in the bed that my sister and I shared. My sister and I shared my brother's single bed and my brother had to sleep on the floor of the bedroom. The two aunts both snored so loud, which kept us all awake. I tried everything to deafen the sound. I eventually went downstairs and tried to sleep on the settee. When I dared to mention it to my mother that I could not sleep due to the snoring she went mental. Something snapped within her, and I received such a beating. The bedroom was so tiny I could not escape her lashing out. The consequence was I told my friend and her mother from church what had happened, and she kindly invited me to stay with them until the visitors had returned to Scotland. This was the same kind lady who had previously taken us in to her home when my mother left my stepfather the previous year.

A Ride Too Far

Whilst I was still at school, my mother worked in a local café. I must have called there one day and was observed by one of the customers. He asked my mother if he could take me out. He must have been at least ten years older than me. I had no say in the matter.

He picked me up at the house in his car and drove me to a river on the outskirts of town. I know I would have found it difficult to initiate conversation, as I always felt uncomfortable with people I did not know. He parked the car and we walked along the riverbank. I remember sitting on the grass and he tried to kiss me. I pushed him away and started to run away but he caught me and started to grab hold of me. Thankfully a dog walker was walking towards us, and he let go of me. I refused to get back in his car. Eventually I did get back into his car and he took me home. I did not tell my mother what had happened. This changed when she told me he was coming to take me out again the following week. I told her I would not go due to what he did. She told me this is what men are like and he would treat me well as he had a good job. She just accepted that he had a right to abuse me, and she felt no inclination to protect me. Even today I cannot comprehend her reasoning especially when I think of my love towards my own daughters and the innate feelings I have to protect and provide for them.

Who Can You Trust?

As discussed previously apart from my mother and auntie I only once told my secret to someone at church who I thought I could trust. She was the leader of a Bible group I attended and was going away to theology school. I remember on one occasion being upset about an issue relating to my home situation. After the class she spent some time and I told her a little about my home situation regarding my stepfather refusing to speak to me. She appeared genuinely concerned. Over the coming weeks she would ask me how things were at home and would say a prayer for me that things would get better. On one occasion I shared with her the sexual abuse I had encountered as a child. She must have shared this with her husband who told other people in the church. Following one Sunday night service, I was offered a lift home by a man who used to drive past the street where I lived. He asked me outright if I had been sexually abused and asked me to share the details with him.

I cannot remember what I said but I do remember being horrified and worried that other people would find out. I still lived with the shame and guilt that I associated with the past abuse, which of course was reinforced by my mother's description of me, "A Dirty Bitch". My past was no longer a secret at church. This was confirmed by two men, who suddenly started taking more than a general interest in me. Writing about it now the thought comes to me that just like there are certain characteristics that a victim of bullying exhibits it is similar to the victims of child sexual abuse. These people target the vulnerable, the unloved, neglected child without an emotional support network. It is not my intention to expose those involved here. Years later I did discover that one church member had been involved with several young girls when they were at a similar age to me. To my knowledge his conduct had never been reported.

The consequence of this was my trust in confiding in others was completely shattered. This resulted in me withdrawing even more and suppressing any attempt to seek help from anyone regarding my childhood abuse. Maybe if I had not experienced the betrayal of trust, I may have sought professional support and this book would not have been written in its present format as a self-help guide.

What the Past Gave Me

No one can encounter so much negativity and not be affected in many ways especially when it is constant during your childhood. Not only were you robbed of love and affection, you, had no self-identity. The focus was on survival, never questioning your needs apart from avoiding confrontation, aiming to be invisible especially in the home. The name of the game was survival.

My childhood gave me more than painful memories. It is also responsible for my unfounded fears and dislike and avoidance of places as the association with them is linked to my childhood and hellish hole. Only recently I have overcome my issue with parks as I mentioned in the introduction. This was achieved by working with my Inner Child. I have never wanted to spend time in a park; much to the detriment of my two daughters. I would avoid taking them to the park when they were little. I never questioned why I did not like parks. The few times I did go to a park I was aware of a deep sadness that would descend on me. I associated it with negativity but did not understand why. During a session when I was conversing with my Inner Child, I realised that when things were unbearable at home and I had nowhere to go I would visit the nearby park. I would spend hours there doing nothing. I would sit alone on a bench and watch and observe other families playing games or taking their dogs for a walk. Longing to be part of a family and feel loved, they appeared so happy whilst I was so sad. So, I associated parks with both sadness and being cold as it was often during the winter months that I spent time there to avoid my stepfather.

Once I acknowledged the reason why parks were negative places due to my childhood experience, and how my Inner Child had previously never been allowed to process painful memories, which had been suppressed within my unconscious mind, I was able to deal with the memory in a positive manner. With this revelation, I can now spend time in a park and not be engulfed by a great sadness. It is not just incidents and places relating to my childhood that take me to my hellish hole, it can also be the spoken word that provokes painful memories.

The Power of the Spoken Word

"Words are powerful—they can either be a healing balm or provoke pain"—Proverbs Chapter 18 verse 21.

It is not only painful memories generated by the actions of others that are suppressed in our subconscious mind, the spoken word, is also instrumental in generating painful memories that are contained within our subconscious mind. If you were brought up in a home where you were constantly criticised and verbally attacked your concept of yourself and your world will be tainted by negativity.

Our negative thoughts become our beliefs, which we carry with us living our lives according to those beliefs. The words that we heard in our childhood become our heart's mantra. We focus on the negative with statements such as, "I am rubbish at dancing", "I am not a good driver" or "I could never get a degree." Someone will have constantly told you that you were not capable of achieving anything and sadly you believed it.

If you have been subjected to hearing constant negative words during your childhood, it not only provides you with an unhealthy connection to your past, it, reinforces your low self- esteem, and negative image of yourself.

Words are also powerful ammunition for keeping you a slave to the past.

An unknown poet wrote

"A careless word may kindle strife, a cruel word may wreck a life,

A bitter word may hate instil, a brutal word may smile and kill,

A gracious word may smooth the way a joyous word may light the day

A timely word may lessen stress, a loving word may heal and bless."

Sticks and stones can break my bones, but words will never hurt me.

A question for you

Can you honestly say that unkind words have never bothered or knocked your confidence and prevented you from achieving what you were capable of doing through believing the negative words to be true?

When a child is developing and making its own judgement of the world, based on socialisation within the family unit, the words the child hears moulds the child's character. If the majority of the words are more negative than positive the child's self-worth and confidence is thwarted along with the ability and necessary skills to live an optimum life.

Whilst I am sure that my mother at some point must have said some kind words to me, I truly cannot remember. What I do remember is the negative words constantly used towards me. 'Dirty Bitch' was the one label that hurt me so much as I explained earlier.

Other negative words I associate with my mother are when I got engaged and we showed her my engagement ring. She said, "That's not an engagement ring, it looks like a dress ring". When she first saw our new home, again her words were so negative. She told me that one day she would have a bigger house than ours it would be at the seaside and have a white fence around it. I feel she saw me as competition. Without realising, she was jealous of me, and what I had achieved.

The point I am trying to make is how negative words can become lodged in our minds for years. The challenge then becomes how we stop believing in them and most importantly how we can detach from them, so they have no hold over us. This is achieved by growing stronger and believing in our own self-worth.

It is not just the detrimental effect of negative words that cause immense problems; it is just as traumatic, especially to a child, when words of love, praise and encouragement are denied; the impact can have devastating effects.

In the book called *The Blessing,* there is a story that clearly demonstrates the power of words and how being denied words of love can result in a child becoming depressed and withdrawn to the point of death. *A Cipher In The Snow* is an educational film based on a true story. A scene from the movie shows a bunch of school children waiting for the school bus on a snowy January morning. The children are interacting with each other playing in the snow except for one little boy standing by himself just staring at the ground. He appears to be invisible to the other children. When the bus arrives all the children rush to get on the bus out of the cold except for Roger, who is the last one to get on the bus. He wearily climbs the bus steps; each step appears to demand so much effort. None of the other children invite him to sit with them. He sits alone with his head bent low. After traveling only a few miles Roger suddenly staggers to his feet dropping his schoolbooks. The bus driver enquires, "What is the matter kid". Roger does not reply. In frustration and concern the bus driver pulls over to the side of the road and opens the door. As Roger descends down the steps he falls and crumples into the snow. The scene ends with the bus driver standing over Roger and the sound of the ambulance can be heard.

Roger died on the way to school, his medical records highlighted no underlying health problems, and the autopsy was unable to establish the cause of his sudden death. It was a teacher who unravelled the mystery and cause, of his death. The teacher discovered that Roger's life had been erased like the writing on a board. His parents had divorced, his mother found a new partner who was resentful of any time she gave to Roger. This resulted in the time he spent with his mother being monitored. Whilst she loved Roger, she was either too busy or intimidated by her new husband to give him any attention. He was pushed away and experienced rejection from both his father following the divorce and now his mother. His schoolwork began to suffer, homework did not appear, or it was late. Eventually his teachers gave up on him and left him to work alone. He began to withdraw from the other children and would not initiate conversation. This resulted in the other children also leaving him alone.

Roger withdrew and retreated into a world of silence. In a short time, everything, and everyone of value to Roger had been lost or taken away from him. With no place of shelter and no words of encouragement this sensitive child was unable to stand the pain.

It was concluded that Roger, was not killed by a disease or physical wounds. He died through the lack of words of love and acceptance. The lack of spoken blessings from family and friends acted as deadly as a cancer. He died alone believing that he was totally alone, unwanted and unworthy of love.

When I was reading about Roger, I became quite emotional. I had been where Roger had stood, on my own watching the other children, it resurfaced the "Hellish Hole." Roger died of neglect, emotional neglect. You may have been given an abundance of material possessions as a child but if you were denied words of love and encouragement you too are in a deprived state as an adult. You need to hear those precious words that you were denied as a child. This can be rectified as we discover how to love our Inner Child, which entails offering positive healing words.

For a minute return to your childhood, think back to your parent's conversations with you. Were the majority positive or negative? Even if they were generally of a positive nature, I am sure you will be able to identify an occasion when their words hit a nerve. If you can recall such a conversation and be able to identify the action taken as a result of the conversation it demonstrates the power of words and the effect it has had on you.

When the Past Dictates the Future

An obsession I have inherited due to my childhood is my fixation on colour coordinating in relation to the clothes I wear. I have to wear matching underwear; I cannot wear colours that do not compliment, each other. I know exactly why it is an issue with me. I guess you may realise the reason too. I was bullied and taunted by the way I was dressed as a child in an array of different colours that clashed and gave me the label of being different. If I feel uncomfortable with what I am wearing it makes me feel insecure and lacking in confidence.

Just take a few minutes right now and ask yourself if there are any obsessions that you have or any ritual or quirks that you carry out. Once you have identified with them ask yourself what is the reason? Why do you have to do them? Why are they so important? How would it make you feel if you did not do them?

Personality Traits

It is acknowledged by several leading psychologists, who have carried out extensive research into personality traits of victims of child sexual abuse, that there are several recognisable personality traits. I easily identified with several of them. From the list identify any traits that are prominent in your life.

Always apologising

I was always saying sorry to others, apologising if I brushed against someone in a shop or a street despite them banging into me, I would say sorry. It was just an automatic response. I would take the blame even when I was not responsible for the action, as I doubted my authority to defend myself. Even, if someone said something, which I knew was wrong regarding general knowledge, I would remain silent. Or if I heard anyone pronouncing words wrongly during a conversation, I would refrain from correcting them.

People Pleaser

Other people's needs were always a priority. My mother's wants had always to be adhered to in an attempt to make her happy. The consequence was that I acted out several different roles as subconsciously I adapted to what I perceived was my role in making others like me or gaining their favour. A big downside to this is losing your own individual identity and not knowing who you are or what your personal needs are.

Frozen of Emotions

Not being able to express healthy emotions such as crying, anger, laughing.

Neglecting own Needs

This was a consequence of not loving myself, seeing myself as unworthy of being loved for being me. If my mother could not love me and care for me, how could I learn to love myself? You need a role model to look up to and learn from.

Addictions and Self-Harm

I never contemplated self-harm or suicide, but I did suffer with eating problems during my twenties. This was an act of control as I was still a victim to my childhood. As a child I remember biting myself in an attempt to take away the emotional pain I was enduring by replacing it with physical pain.

Fearful

I still lack confidence in several areas. A big one for me, as I previously explained, is driving; I am challenged on the motorway and worry that entering the motorway the traffic will not let me in, which actually did happen once, and I ended up on the hard shoulder. My husband is sometimes critical of my driving. Whilst this is true of most couples, for me it has a greater effect despite having advanced driving lessons and being told that there is nothing wrong with my driving.

Rejection

There are lots of incidents where I have experienced rejection and each time it happens it takes me straight back to my childhood to the place where no one wanted me—my Hellish Hole. Many times, the feelings of rejection have been unfounded especially with my mother-in-law, who was an amazing person and a powerful role model for me.

I knew that my in law's initially did not approve of me, and

I can understand why. They were church going people who thought their son would marry within the church. I was only seventeen when they first met me, and my parents were not Christians. When we got engaged my mother-in-law's shock could not be contained, her words were hurtful. No congratulations or hugs, she just said "What about Wendy, she was a nice a girl". I presume my mother-in-law had expected they would eventually marry. Having now had children of my own I can appreciate how she must have felt when we got engaged. Her only son engaged to a young girl outside the church family and whose mother had been married twice and was now co-habiting. I was even told by my husband's auntie that the family were concerned about my husband because as the saying goes "Like mother like daughter".

Helping others as avoidance of own needs

This is a common trait in many therapists and those who work in the care industry. By focusing on the needs of others they block out their own pain, trying to convince themselves their own pain is nothing compared to those they are administering to. This is just a coping strategy. It is true you can always find someone who has endured so much more than you but it's the damage the incidents have caused to the individual not the classification of the violation that is the issue.

Making Decisions

Being so indecisive in relation to both major and small decisions caused by fear of making the wrong choice. Resulting in feeling responsible, for the consequences of that decision.

Trusting Others

Doubting people's motives when they demonstrate kindness

towards you. Questioning if they have hidden agendas. Not responding well to compliments and praise, despite a genuine need to be acknowledged and appreciated.

A question for you

As you read the above traits what thoughts surfaced? Could you identify with the majority of them? Maybe go back to the traits and write down how each one of them manifests in your life. You really do not need to accept your life as it is. You can implement change. It only takes one tiny step to start the process. Start to bring about change and be free of the past with its pain and shame like I did.

When all these traits were evident in my life, I existed as a robot, devoid of emotion and feelings, running on a pre-installed program. The latter was a collection of beliefs I was convinced to be true of myself. The program was installed and maintained by the reaction of adults mainly my mother. I continued to treat myself the same way my mother treated me, which resulted in the inability to love myself.

That was until I read Louise Hay's book You Can Heal Your Life. This was another catalyst for change in my life. I wish I could say that I have conquered all the negative traits I inherited, but truthfully, I have not, it is a work in progress. However, I do now possess the key to continue my healing journey. It is to continue to **love myself** through working with my Inner Child which gives me all the tools required to bring about changes in my mind, body and spirit.

> *It is now safe for me to release all of my childhood traumas and move into love*—Louise Hay

Louise Lynn Hay is my role model. She was born on the 8th, October 1926, she is a renowned motivational author and founder of Hay House Publishing Company. She has written several self-help books including You Can Heal Your Life, which was first written in 1984. The book sold 50 million copies around the world and has been published in over 30 languages.

It was through attending the First Church of Religious Science she was introduced to the transformative power of thoughts, claiming that positive thinking could change people's material circumstances and heal the body. She became a Religious Science Practitioner in the early 1970s and promoted the use of daily affirmations, which she believed would cure their illnesses.

In the late 1970s she was diagnosed with incurable cervical cancer, she came to the conclusion that by holding on to her resentment concerning her childhood abuse and rape, she had contributed to the onset of the cancer. Refusing conventional medicine, she began a regime of forgiveness and embarked upon a program of holistic therapies including reflexology and colon hydrotherapy.

I immediately related to Louise Hay. She had experienced a childhood not dissimilar to my own. On her healing journey she embraced a lot of the therapies that I am involved with. She also embarked on a cleansing detoxing regime, which I too am passionate about, and promoting the virtues of sound therapy that she uses in her guided meditations.

At the beginning of her book, she clearly states some points of her philosophy:

We are each responsible for all our experiences

Every thought we think is creating our future

The point of power is always in the present moment

Everyone suffers from self-hatred and guilt

The bottom line for everyone is, "I am not good

114

enough"

It's only a little thought and a thought can be changed

We create every so-called illness in our body

Resentment, criticism and guilt are the most dangerous patterns

We must release the past and forgive everyone

We must be willing to learn to love ourselves

Self-approval and self-acceptance in the now are the keys to positive change

When we really love ourselves, everything in our lives works.

It would be impossible within the constraints of my book to explore all of her philosophies. I have chosen to focus briefly on the philosophies that I related to and adopted in my healing journey. They form a thread that runs through my book. I do urge you to purchase her book at some point to study in detail her philosophies and learn that you too already possess the tools to heal your own life.

My Healing Journey

Following my Coming Out on the 19th September 2012, when I told my mother I was not a dirty bitch I have been on a remarkable journey. I became aware that the past had influenced every aspect of my life and only I could implement change. As crazy as it sounds it meant leaving my comfort zone, addressing my deep-rooted fears and being willing to change. This was both challenging and rewarding. From that day life took on a new dimension.

On my journey I truly believe that I have been guided. Too many times the right words have been said just at the right time guiding me to explore a new concept or a book has been recommended which has been a source of knowledge and encouragement. As I have shared my aspiration for the book several clients and two friends have identified with my childhood as they have been sexually abused and neglected or had narcissistic mothers.

I have a plaque, which was given to me over forty years ago. At the time I did not fully realise the truth of those words.

Every experience that God gives you,

Every person He puts in your life

Is in preparation for the future that only He can see.

I totally believe that to be true, I have learnt so much from others along with childhood experiences, which has been both the inspiration and motivation to share my healing journey through the pages of this book.

Let the Healing Begin

Regarding your personal journey, the first thing you need to do is take responsibility for your own life, just as I did and commit to a program of change. For me this included:

Changing my thought patterns

I became aware of the influence that negative thoughts had on me. I had used the concept of the Law of Attraction on many occasions. I believe it was responsible for selling a house. Despite the recession within weeks, we had two buyers and received almost the full asking price.

The same philosophy was extended to my thought patterns; whatever we think about ourselves becomes true. I was reinforcing my negativity towards myself; each time I told myself it was my fault or that I was unlovable. It had to stop. My thoughts were keeping me anchored to the past. Our words and thoughts create our experiences. As the subconscious mind accepts whatever we chose to believe is true.

Blame is a no-win game

We live in a blame society; people often find it hard to say sorry and admit that something is their fault and they are responsible. They blame anyone and anything rather than take responsibility for their actions. When I commenced my healing journey, I attributed blame to my parents especially my mother. If she had been able to love me and protect me my childhood would have been so different, or so I believed. Working with my Inner Child along with extensive reading and various healing therapies, I came to realise that blaming others achieves nothing. It's like super glue, it keeps you stuck in the victim role. In blaming another we give our power away, understanding allows you to rise above the problem. The past is gone, and nothing can ever be achieved by remaining stuck and frozen.

I can now accept that my parents were just hurting individuals, who were not happy, they were angry, frustrated and searching for love themselves. I can see this in the way they both had extra marital relations, looking outside of themselves for love and acceptance. In relation to my mother, you will remember that my grandmother became pregnant prior to getting married. This resulted in my grandma leaving her hometown and moving to Lancashire. I can imagine that she would have encountered many obstacles and possibly resentment towards her unborn baby. This negative energy may have caused my mother subconsciously to believe that she was unwanted and unloved, despite my grandparents being so kind and caring to her grandchildren. You will never be free from the past until you become a member of The No Blame Game.

Letting Go of The Past

If we are unable to live in the present moment and often revisit the past it is a sign that we are stuck, when you are stuck it means that nothing flows in the present moment. The antidote is to let go. I have witnessed many times individual clients letting go during a colonic treatment as the body commences to release its toxic waste. It can coincide with an emotional release as tears flow and lots of anger and hurt is released. The same reaction can happen during a Sound Massage treatment or Reiki. What follows is a more positive approach to problems, along with a new- found strength.

Forgiveness is a major component of your healing journey. The essential ingredient to forgiveness is LOVE, which needs to come from your heart, starting with yourself. There are several ways you can start the process when working with your Inner Child included in Part Three.

Thoughts are just thoughts, and you can change them

It is worth emphasising again, '*You are what you think*'. Your thoughts mould your life. Have you noticed that when you have a negative thought about yourself it is linked to a negative feeling? Change the thought and the feeling will go away. The point of power is in the moment so you can change your negative thoughts right now. I worked with this concept of changing negative thoughts by choosing thoughts that were nurturing and by learning to love myself, whilst building up my self-esteem. This was achieved by mirror work, which is explained in Part Four. Your mind is a tool, to use in any way you decide. You control your mind and thoughts.

Learning that we don't have to continually strive for perfection

I had always set very high standards for myself and other people as I felt that I was constantly being judged by my actions. It was often an attempt to gain the praise and appreciation that I had been searching for in my childhood. I would become obsessed with perfection and if not achieved I would feel a failure, which in turn reinforced my childhood belief that I was a dirty bitch and a lazy bitch, words that were infused in my mind. Once I started to address my negative thoughts and replace them with words of encouragement, I not only started to feel better, I developed more patience with myself and adopted a more gentle approach to my Inner Child. I realised that my Inner Child had for so long been subjected to abuse, and that I had continued to abuse her. The notion came to me, that you would not shout and demand that a small child would be able to accomplish tasks instantly. By relating to myself as a small child, I was able to have a, more gentle approach to myself, and allow imperfections not to have the same impact as previously. The fact that this book has been published is proof in itself that I have come to terms with my imperfections.

Learning to love myself

I realised that this was the most important thing I could ever do, by learning to love myself all the other traits would automatically change. I started the process by working with my Inner Child.

A question for you

So where do you start your healing journey? What is the first step to becoming free from the past? For me it was to connect with my Inner Child. According to Louise Hay "It doesn't matter how old you are, there is a little child within who needs love and acceptance. If you are a woman, no matter how self-reliant you are, you have a little girl who's very tender and needs your help. If you are a man no matter how macho you are, you still have a little boy inside you who craves warmth and affection."

Let's now explore the whole concept of the Inner Child and discover ways to connect to that little child who resides within you.

Part Three

The Inner Child

I am a child, get me out of here

A question for you

How does the whole concept of an Inner Child existing within you resonate? Does this child really exist? Or is it simply a psychological term attempting to explain why many adults exhibit childlike behaviour or suffer from mental illness because as a child they were traumatised or neglected?

During my journey of recovery and researching the Inner Child for the purpose of this book I have read many books and articles. Although they described the concept adequately, they did not instantly enable me to identify or understand what they were trying to explain. This was despite having worked with my Inner Child through various healing therapies. The more research I carried out, gathering many psychological definitions, the more elusive the whole concept of the Inner Child became. It could have been due to the terminology used or the presumption that the reader had a substantial knowledge base of the subject.

As I mentioned previously, I am not setting myself up as an expert in anything, I acknowledge that you may have a more in-depth knowledge of the theory of the Inner Child. I have adopted an approach that aims to benefit the reader who has little or no knowledge of the Inner Child, ensuring that it is not too difficult to understand.

The Inner Child is also referred to as "divine child", "wonder child", "true self" or the "child within". The Inner Child refers to a part of the adult personality that houses childlike and adolescent behaviour, emotions, habits, attitudes and thought patterns. It is viewed as an autonomous sub-personality with its own needs, desires and goals. It can therefore function independently to the adult self, resulting in inner turmoil and opposition to the more mature adult personality.

The Inner Child can be seen as falling into defined characteristics.

Abandoned Child

This child feels very lonely, insecure and unwanted and craves attention and safety. Fears of being abandoned continue into adulthood even throughout a secure marriage. Busy divorced or separated parents are often the main reason why the Inner Child exhibits these, often unfounded, fears.

Neglected Child

This Inner Child is expressed through a depressed and withdrawn adult. Not having received love and affection from parents during childhood, they do not know how to express love and feel unworthy of receiving love. They grow up into adults who do not know how to love themselves.

Playful Child

This Inner Child is relatively happy and is emotionally healthy. They know how to be happy and have fun. They are in touch with their creativity.

Spoilt Child

This child tends to have an elevated self-image. They are likely to display uncontrolled anger, have tantrums when their needs and desires are not immediately met.

Fearful Child

This Inner Child is always filled with fear and anxiety, which can cause panic attacks. During childhood they received a lot of criticism from parents or care givers. They constantly need to hear words of encouragement.

Disconnected Child

This Inner Child is probably the most damaged and hurting. In childhood they were made to feel invisible and generally ignored. In adulthood this is displayed in not being able to trust others and having problems with relationships as they have never experienced being close to anyone and have not experienced unconditional love. They prefer to stay isolated and detached. They are very fearful and avoid any new experiences. They need constant loving attention and support to feel of any value.

The list above is just a brief outline of the characteristics associated to the various Inner Child personalities. It is said that we each have more than one Inner Child that resides within us. As you read the characteristics it is possible that you related to more than one of them. We all progress through a series of developmental steps from infancy to childhood to adolescence to adulthood. If this progression is not structured and vital elements of development are not achieved part of us simply stops growing. This damaged, wounded part of us becomes an Inner Child who is trapped in that stage of growth.

So be prepared to meet more than one aspect of your Inner Child on your journey. As you connect with him or her, are you for example:

The infant child who demanded attention and physical contact and was denied these basic needs?

The two years old, toddler who was never allowed to display anger.

The eight years old who was sexually abused.

The fifteen years old who felt fat and ugly which was reinforced by parents or carers.

These "children" who are cocooned within your adult self, are waiting for the opportunity to be loved and given a voice to express their deep-rooted pain.

As we learn to parent our own damaged Inner Child and take into account how behaviour is linked to child development stages many behaviour traits will change. For example, if we can relate to our infant self in a therapeutic and loving manner the adult behaviour pattern of needing constant attention could diminish. Or by working with our repressed toddler's need for exploration and independence, the fear of taking risks will lessen allowing you to accept challenges and attain success.

There are many excellent resources available, several, which I have used personally, are listed in the references at the end of the book. An excellent workbook by Cathryn L Taylor provides you with more tools to work with your inner child as does the work of Beverly Engel.

There are also other activities for you to work with in Part Four. It is essential to understand that working with the Inner Child can be extremely demanding. It requires commitment along with the motivation to want to change learnt behaviour patterns. It is said that through working with our Inner Child we find our spirit. According to Erik Erikson "The greatest sin of all is the mutilation of the child spirit. If the spirit of a child is allowed to grow, then the child can make decisions that promote life and trust. For those raised in dysfunctional families it is the path towards sanity"

I quote the words of a leading pioneer in the field of the Inner Child work, Charles L. Whitfield in his book A Gift to Myself.

Who am I?

Our child within is who we really are-

Ultimately alive, energetic, creative and fulfilled.

After we remove all the masks, facades, trappings and superficialities of who

we may have thought we were

and who we may have needed to be to survive

what remains is our True Self, Our Real Self

- our Child Within.

But to survive a difficult childhood,

And for some people even a dangerous childhood,

And adolescence, our child within went into hiding.

The pain and confusion were just too great for it.

Even though our child within

May have gone into hiding, it never dies.

It is always there, waiting

To peep its small head,

Sometimes with big eyes, and

Usually with an open heart,

Out into life.

It wants to be, to experience,

To create and evolve.

It wants to feel connected, to be part of life.

The world, and the universe.

When we discover and remember

This core of our identity,

We begin our healing journey and adventure.

Psychological theories tend to portray the Inner Child through words presented in theory books and research papers, which need processing in the mind. Reading the poem for me contains the true essence of my Inner Child, which resonates with both my mind but more importantly with my heart.

Cathryn L. Taylor in her book asks, "Who are the Inner Children within? Simply they are the voices inside you that you were not able to express as a child".

Throughout my healing journey working with my Inner Child, I have only been able to share some of the activities with individuals who are on a similar journey to myself, as I feel that whilst it is of vital importance in many areas of emotional health, it appears to be an area that is not discussed, hence the subject of Inner Child is shrouded in mystery and ridicule.

Discovering my Inner Child was instrumental in my healing journey; it was the key that enabled me to discover who I really was and not the person I thought I was. Children who have been sexually abused or have experienced a challenging background, rarely have a strong recognition of themselves. In order to be independent of the past and be in control of our lives and destiny, we need to find our true selves not the person we have become in order to live with the past, **the real you, the true you.** This will be achieved through acknowledging your likes and dislikes, becoming aware of your values and finding your individual blue- print.

By carrying out self-discovery activities and connecting to your Inner Child you will create an inner awareness of who you really are.

The activities listed below are an attempt to make you question your identity, do you truly own the characteristics or traits you display to others or do they just serve as a mask to hide your true self, your Inner Child. **You do not have to work through every activity to reveal the truth.** Deep inside you know your Inner Child, you know who you really are and what you came into this world capable of achieving. You now need to learn to re-connect to reveal your true self and reach your full potential.

The majority of the activities have been slightly modified from the work of Beverly Engel, a prominent American therapist has worked extensively with victims of sexual abuse, she has given me permission, to print, the following activities.

> *I love myself enough to go beyond my parent's limitations*—Louise Hay

Who are you?

Activity One

Either mentally note or write down who you are. You can start with your name but that doesn't describe you; it's just a name your parents gave you. Yes, you are a person, a statistic along with the rest of the population, but does that describe you? The majority of people when asked that question will describe themselves in a role such as wife, mother, daughter or son. Or they will identify themselves as a nurse, accountant, computer programmer but so are millions of people working in the same professions or jobs. Does that make YOU?

Activity Two

Write down the number of roles you undertake in your life. You may be surprised at how many different roles you juggle meeting demands of others. These are superficial to your inner self. They do not describe who you really are.

How would you describe your personality or character? Are you confident, shy, serious or independent? What about your feelings are you happy, angry, depressed or content? Why do you identify with that personality, is it really you? Or is it what you have been socialised into by your parents? In sociology the term nature or nurture debate exists. It describes how an individual's personality is formed. Do you act in a certain way due to your upbringing, socialisation, or is it recorded in your DNA, genetic makeup.

Activity Three

Write down the personalities of your parents or other individuals who were responsible for caring for you as a child. Note both their good and bad points that describe them. Aim to identify at least four traits. This activity will give you the opportunity to compare and contrast your personality against your parent's, which is important in your quest to discover the real you.

My list

My parents divorced when I was twelve. My father showed little interest in me, or my siblings. Several years later he announced he wasn't my biological father. It was therefore not easy to write down his characteristics, as I do not feel I ever had the opportunity to get to know him intimately.

My Father

Four Traits that I would use to describe him are:
- Reliable in the work situation,
- Intelligent (he went to a grammar school,)
- Cruel and violent towards both my mother, brother and me
- Dishonest; had several affairs before my parents divorced.

My Mother

- Cruel, angry and violent,
- Unhappy and depressed,
- Lazy in household tasks
- Jealousy towards most people.

I believe that because my mother displayed narcissistic tendencies, she was incapable of displaying any of the virtues that you would expect of a loving mother.

What have I inherited from my parents? To be honest the desire to be nothing like them.

However, in terms of discovering my true self the fact that I avoided being identified with my parents was a barrier to discovering my true self, as I avoided any personality that surfaced in me that I believed was a reflection of my parents. This had the same consequences as if I had a strong desire to be like them. On both accounts I would still be governed by them, which was detrimental in discovering my true self. Interestingly both my sister and I have an obsession for housework almost to the point of having, Obsessive Compulsive Disorder (OCD).

A question for you

What does your list say about you? Can you identify both the positive and negative traits that you have inherited from your parents? Remember you are not your parents, You Are You.

Activity Four

Now list all the traits that make you different from your parents. Why do you think you developed these qualities? It will make you realise why you act the way you do. If your list contains negative traits, such as anger, you do not have to accept you have an angry disposition, you can work on the anger ensuring that you do not pass this on to others like your parents have done to you.

Activity Five

At this point I would like you to revisit a childhood memory of someone who you believe influenced your life. By wanting to be like them, you reflected some of their personality traits. It may have been a teacher, a family member, a character from a book, a movie star, pop star, neighbour or someone you admired and used as a role model. If it was an individual, you had personal contact with try for a few seconds to recall an incident where this person demonstrated a genuine act of love towards you. It would be beneficial to write about the occasion and how it influenced your life. Do not worry if the task appears too difficult at the moment. It can be difficult for some people to identify with their feelings as they are emotionally blocked. It is enough to just recall any person who helped you in a positive way during your childhood.

As you work with your Inner Child it is envisaged that you will be able to revisit your childhood and the trauma associated with the past will become less destructive as you free your Inner Child. By allowing memories to surface and seeing both the positive and negative aspects of your childhood it will allow you to become aware of your feelings. How did the incident make you feel? Try and notice how calm and still you feel as your heart expands in love and gratitude towards that special person. You cannot feel both sad and happy or angry and peaceful at the same time. Also become aware of how powerful memories are and how they remain in your subconscious mind. I would encourage you to occasionally try and revisit your childhood, remembering an incident and observing the emotion it contains, in an attempt to connect to your suppressed feelings.

Returning to your special person, list their qualities, why did they make you aspire to be like them? Pop stars, celebrities, what did you like about them? their music? the way they dressed? Notice how celebrities are used in marketing products and how the sales of the product escalate due to individuals wanting to identify with that person. On a smaller scale it is the same with people we admire. We see something in them that we want to aspire to.

Mrs Bell was my primary school teacher, she walked to school each day. My brother and I would wait for her, and we would walk with her to school. She was always kind to us realising probably due to our clothes and the occasional bruises that we did not have a happy home. She made me aware that I had a talent for writing; she would send me to another class to read my stories to the pupils and teacher. She constantly praised me and told me to work hard at school, which I did. Being with her made me feel special, she was the kindest teacher I ever encountered, all the children loved her. I never saw her get angry. I used to wish she were my mother. I believe that her influence inspired me to work hard at school and to believe that I had the ability to succeed.

Whilst you may have had limited positive role models as a child, you need to identify with the people you admire or want to aspire to. It does not matter what age you are. Your Inner Child still needs to grow and develop. You will never become identical to your role models. Just cherry pick their traits or qualities that you wish to aspire to, which will be unique and personal to you. It is about opening up your horizons and discovering yourself and unleashing your full potential.

Activity Six

Make a list of all the words your parents used to describe you. Mine would include "dirty bitch", "lazy bitch," "religious bitch", "promiscuous", "liar" to name a few. My father use to call me "Poppet", a name I cherished for many years.

Analyse your list and cross out the statements that are not true about you, highlight the ones that you believe are true. From the list divide into the ones that are positive and the ones that are negative. If your list now contains more negative traits than positive, assess the negatives; were they essential for you to survive as a child in a dysfunctional family? An example would be telling lies.

Another consideration when looking at your list is that a trait, for example being stubborn, that your parents labelled you with could be interpreted as assertive, which is not a negative trait. If there are features of your personality that are true, which you would like to change, you have the power within to achieve that, to sever from the past. You are stronger than what you realise, remember you have survived a challenging childhood.

Another revelation I discovered was how the words of influential people in your childhood can have an impact on your future. Prior to my parents divorcing my father told me "Never change". At the time I did not fully understand the connotation of his words. Now I question if deep within my subconscious mind, I resisted change, which was detrimental, preventing me from discovering earlier my true self, as I was still seeking love and affection from my father by acting in a way that I thought would please him.

Can you identify a certain behaviour pattern that has its roots from the words you heard as a child?

I suggest you work on one trait at a time. For example, you

may have identified that you have a jealous streak. Maybe you are jealous of friends, who appears to have a better income than you, go on more holidays, have a better car, home, or a sibling who has higher qualifications than you which makes you feel inferior.

Create an affirmation that focuses on you and not on others.

> *Positive affirmations are becoming a positive habit for me*—Louise Hay

I have within myself all I need to make me happy

I am happy with what the universe provides for me

I have all I need to make today a good day

I have the power to achieve great things

Write them down and repeat them until you believe it. Or select just one or better still write your own and throughout the day repeat it.

Now write down two lists one headed STRENGTHS and the other WEAKNESSES

I suspect that you will have a longer list of weaknesses than strengths, finding it difficult to list your strengths. This is probably due to your parents giving you a negative self-image and ignoring your innate qualities. I suggest you ask a close friend to identify some of the strengths they see in you.

In her book The Right To Innocence, Beverly Engel states that the reason why we have lost connection to our Inner Child is by our parents instilling into us commandments:

- Don't trust others

134

- Don't tell others about what goes on in the family

- Don't question authority

- Don't listen to or respect your body

- Don't get angry or assert yourself

- Don't think for yourself

- Don't reveal yourself

- Don't take care of yourself

- Don't ask for help.

Do you identify with any of the commandments? How many of them are still influencing your life? Engel encourages you to reject any of the commandments that you no longer believe to be true. Not all of the commandments are false; some are valid and practical. By eliminating the ones that are not true you can create a new set of beliefs grounded on the positive messages, which promotes and identifies your true personality and qualities

The principle behind all the activities is to demonstrate that the majority of people do not know who they really are. They hide themselves within roles characters and feelings that are preventing them from being true to their real selves.

Your Emotions—The Key to Your True Self.

The way to reveal your true self is to connect with your emotions and feelings. This is often not an easy thing for adults, who have experienced sexual abuse, as we have learnt how to deny our true feelings in an attempt to survive and conform to the demands of our complex environment. Often basic emotions such as laughing, crying, anger and joy are not naturally exhibited. We have learnt to restrain our natural response, which comes at a great price as it is through our feelings that are expressed as an emotion that we connect to our true self, our Inner Child.

A question for you

Stop reading right now and ask yourself how do I feel right now? Not easy, is it? It is often more difficult than knowing what you want. We have lost the skill of considering our own needs, just like we have lost the skill to exhibit our feelings. If the way you are feeling is not easily identified, what do you NOT feel? Do you feel angry right now, or fearful; are you sad or are you happy? Do you feel nothing? Are you emotionally shut down like I used to be? You feel nothing and you are on automatic pilot, and you just exist?

  Throughout the day check in to your feelings. Make a conscious effort to ask yourself "How do I feel right now?' Write the feeling down in your journal. In the morning before you get out of bed ask yourself 'how do I feel today?' The philosophy underpinning this is whatever you are feeling is exactly what you will bring into your life that day. (The Law of Attraction, which will be covered in more detail in Part Four.) If you wake up each morning feeling irritable you will encounter issues throughout the day, which will keep you in that state of mind. Everything has a frequency, people, places, flowers, crystals, the weather, everything that you can see right now has a frequency. This includes our feelings. So negative feelings will attract more negative feelings. It is a law just like the law of gravity.

It is so important to acknowledge your emotions and feelings. Every time feelings are denied they are suppressed, which prevents you from discovering your true self. You are alienating yourself from your true self, your Inner Child.

Activating your Senses

Another area I feel needs to be highlighted, is that sexually abused children also shut down their senses, sight, sound, taste and touch as an attempt to detach from the trauma that is being inflicted on them.

This fact was brought to my attention in a beautiful way. A friend took me to a garden at a Buddhist's monastery. Once we located a seat, she left me and started to wander around the garden. She had previously attended retreats at the monastery and wanted to look for some herbs that she had planted. When she returned, +she asked what I had seen? My initial reaction was that I had seen nothing. My friend told me that she had been observing me from a distance. Whilst I had sat there a bird had been busy bringing twigs and branches to build a nest in a tree only a few feet from where I sat. She then asked me if I had seen two butterflies on a buddleia bush, or had I seen the sheep on the hillside. She enquired if I had heard the monastery clock strike 3pm, which I had heard. She then asked if I had heard the birds in the trees and the two birds that flew overhead. I had not heard the birds or the sound of the wind in the trees or the gentle noise of water coming from a fountain behind me. Once she had mentioned the water fountain I could hear it, if I listened. The point my friend was trying to make with me is that the majority of people do not use all the senses—something deep within them is switched off and they miss out on all the beauty of creation.

I cannot say that the reason why I did not activate my senses, was due to my childhood past, but it did make me think and become more aware of the gift of our senses and use them to observe the beauty of creation.

A good way of developing your hearing is to listen to music, which is a very therapeutic tool. Try listening to the lyrics of a song. Try to identify how many different musical instruments are contained within the track of the music. Touch is also a powerful way to activate your senses. This may be an area, which up to now has been avoided for obvious reasons. Touch is a healing therapy; if you have someone close that you can trust ask them to gently massage your back or if that is too intimate ask them to massage your feet. Consider having a professional massage or reflexology treatment. Whatever you decide, focus on the sensation of touch. What do different fabrics feel like when you touch them? What is the difference between leather and cotton wool or wood and metal?

Another challenge for you to attempt to activate your senses is to really observe the next person you see. Notice if they are wearing jewellery, what colour are their shoes, what colour are their eyes, their hair? Are they wearing perfume? Now look around you at all the different colours, how many can you observe in a minute? How many different shades of blue are there? Observe the variation of green all around you. You will be surprised how many colour variations there are when you make a conscious effort to really look.

Colour therapy is an amazing discovery; you can wear different colours to activate feel good factors within you. The way your senses perceive your environment is an indicator of your world. The environment can influence your day. We associate happiness with warm sunny days and not so happy days with dark damp days when it never gets really light. For some individuals they do not need the weather as a barometer to achieve happiness and activate the feel-good factor. I have a special friend who says there is no such thing as bad weather;

it's just a bad choice of clothing. We should not let the weather influence us. There are others who do not pay any attention to the weather for a different reason. They are so detached from their true self, so emotionally shut down or depressed, that nothing has any effect on them. They are numb to the world and themselves.

> *Loving myself is the most important thing I can ever do. I deserve to live a good life and I begin now*—Louise Hay

It is now time for you to make a commitment to yourself and start to love yourself more than you have loved anyone. Forget the infatuated love that sweeps you off your feet for a time. The love and respect you need to give yourself will last a lifetime as you learn not only to love yourself but to love others and to love life itself.

It is hoped that you have formed an awareness of your Inner Child. However precarious, just by accepting that there may be an element of truth in the concept of the Inner Child is the first step. Until your Inner Child starts to trust you and open up to you the relationship will have been all one way, with you being the one who is initiating everything. One thing your Inner Child is initially incapable of doing is trusting you. In fact, trusting anyone. Remember all the things we have discussed previously, how you were damaged due to your childhood trauma along with your parents' code of behaviour. With this in mind your Inner Child simply is not going to run to you with open arms. They need you to demonstrate that you love them. The following activities will help you build up a closer relationship with them.

Looking After Number One

This is something that does not come naturally to many people. The innate role of a mother is to provide and care for her family often at the expense of themselves. I witness this often in the clinic as mothers stop coming for treatments due to financial issues within the family with children wanting to go on school trips overseas, driving lessons and family holidays, etc. We sacrifice our needs and neglect ourselves, feeling selfish if we place our own interests before those of the rest of the family. For those from a dysfunctional family self-sacrificing for our family can be even more intense as we try to give our children everything we were denied as children. We make good care givers.

Research shows that a high percentage of those employed in the care sector have grown up in dysfunctional families. We anticipate the needs of others to the point of self-sacrifice.

As children of a dysfunctional family, we were not taught the basic principles of how to care for ourselves, by example or by teaching. If we expressed our needs to our parents, they were more often ignored and rejected. You then stop asking, you held back your needs considering them not important within the family unit. Your instinct was to survive, which meant being as unobtrusive as possible, so just like you did with your feelings you had to suppress your needs.

Self-love helps me make positive changes easily—Louise Hay

On your journey of recovery, the next stage can be an enormous one. You need to really start to learn to **love yourself**, which for me was a real challenge. You are learning to let go of so much, the past, the stigma, the negative thoughts. They need to be replaced with positive healthy habits and beliefs. These virtues will become much easier to accomplish when you start to love yourself and believe that you deserve to have your needs met and not be sacrificed for others. I am not advocating that you adopt a selfish attitude, only that you create a more balanced approach in considering the needs of others along with your own. This poses another question for many "What are my needs?" They have been denied for so long that they do not come easily to the forefront. We may constantly strive to meet the needs of others out of love and the desire to make them happy. In relation to your own needs what makes you happy and feeds your spirit your true self your inner child.

The relationship with your Inner Child may be vague and distant, however the fact that you are still reading the book is an achievement in itself. Whilst this may not be the time for you to fully commit to your personal journey of recovery is totally acceptable, your sub-conscious mind will have retained the essence of the book and the message it contains. You may start to realise that you feel less anxious, or you start to question your actions as to the reason why you react to certain situations. You may find you have more positive thoughts than negative thoughts. You adopt the glass looks half full and not half empty philosophy, without making a conscious decision your thought forms are changing as your frequency is changing and you are attracting positive things into your life.

When I first started trying to connect to my Inner Child it felt totally superficial. I tried the meditation CDs but would fall asleep in the middle of them, or my mind would wander off making me frustrated, and feeling like a failure. I decided to play Inner Child meditations at night when going to sleep playing them through my phone and Pillow Talk, which is an excellent device that allows you to listen to music through a tiny speaker that sits inside your pillow.

Whilst working with my Inner Child I suddenly noticed that my hair had started to part in the middle of my head just like I used to wear it when I was a young child. I had not had a centre parting since I was fifteen when I left school and started work.

But brushing my hair back it would naturally part down the middle. Also, whilst working on the Inner Child activities I unintentionally started to suck my thumb, something I had done when I was young. I cannot say with any authority that it was due to working with my Inner Child, however it is said by Deepak Chopra, that our cells hold memories. (We will explore the concept of cellular memories in Part Four)

For those of you who now feel that you seriously want to connect to your Inner Child you need to establish some promises that you are going to make to your Inner Child, your true self.

Things to consider for your list of promises are:
- To make your needs a priority
- Make decisions without fearing the consequences
- Ask for things you want, refusing to do what you do not want to do
- Treat yourself occasionally because you deserve it
- Praise yourself when you accomplish something on your journey
- Spend time on your own searching for your true identity
- Acknowledging that you have choices and rights
- Work on your self-image by changing things that you do not like about yourself
- Give yourself permission to change
- Demonstrate acts of independence if that has been an issue with you
- Learn to say no and mean it.
- Nurture yourself and indulge yourself
- Laugh often, play more.

The list is not exhaustive; you can add other promises that are unique to you. It does however give you a basic framework for you to expand upon. I would encourage you to make some realistic promises that you have a chance of accomplishing.

My twelve promises to Poppet

(Poppet is the name I call my Inner Child).
- I will acknowledge you everyday

142

- I will remember to ask for what I need
- I will make decisions and become less indecisive
- I will stop being a constant people pleaser
- I will stop saying sorry when it is not my fault
- I will become less fearful of the future
- I will treat myself without feeling guilty
- I will trust myself, and others more
- I will allow myself to cry
- I will demonstrate love towards myself
- I will adopt a more positive attitude towards change
- I will start wearing brighter colours

To acknowledge my Inner Child every day, on my desk I have a photograph of myself when I was around nine. I often tell my Inner Child that I am sorry that she had endured so much hurt and negativity in her life. But I will never allow her to suffer again. I always thank her for sacrificing her childhood and through her sacrificial love she had made me the person I am today.

> *Within myself I see a loving, beautiful being, it is safe for me to look within*—Louise Hay

Value

Along with learning to love yourself, it is essential to your recovery that you also start to value yourself. If you do not learn to do this, you will find that others both in the home and in the work environment won't either. Many of us were never encouraged to value ourselves throughout our childhood. Therefore, it is no wonder we do not attribute any value or worth to ourselves.

We need to start to value ourselves, which involves loving ourselves, by valuing our time, energy and nurturing our bodies. The Inner Child Detox in Part Four, will provide tools to perform practical acts of love, as you learn to nurture and care for yourself in a way that you have never encountered. This will increase your feelings of worth and value instilling confidence in yourself, as you start to respond to the tender loving care you deserve.

You also need to surround yourself with positive people who value you and are supportive. Start to question the motives of your friends and colleagues. Do they support you? Do you genuinely feel relaxed in their company? Do they leave you feeling exhausted as if they had drained all your energy? Are they emotionally zapping you with their negative attitude? It is time to seriously consider being open to new friendships and relationships. You are in the realms of change and the confidence you will start to experience, certainly will be encouraged from those who genuinely care and will encourage you to become the person you are capable of becoming.

Inner Child Activities

I keep my Inner Child happy, and
I am happy too—Louise Hay

The following activities are taken from Beverly Engel's book. As previously stated, you are not expected to embark on every activity listed. Just select the activity or activities that resonate with you. Whilst they are not guaranteed to immediately open the door of your heart towards your Inner Child. They are positive first steps to take on your journey of discovery. They do however need a commitment from you to make them work and need to be approached in a respectful way.

Activity One

Find a quiet place where you will not be disturbed and take a soft cuddly toy and start to tenderly stroke the toy. Close your eyes and imagine that the toy is your Inner Child. Speak softly and tenderly to your Inner Child. Tell them that you are always going to protect them, that you will look after them and never allow anyone to hurt them or abuse them again.
It may feel uncomfortable and awkward at first, but be patient, stay there at least five minutes, tell your Inner Child that you will continue to be there for them telling them when you will next come into their presence and connect with them again.
If you don't have a cuddly toy or you want to make it special go and buy a new soft toy. Think about the type of toy you want; it may be a stuffed toy that you remember when you were young, a rabbit a teddy bear, or lamb. Or you may decide that caressing a soft toy is something that doesn't feel right then please use a pillow or cushion, anything that allows you physically to demonstrate a loving caring attitude towards

you Inner Child.

Activity Two

Find a photograph of yourself when you were a child, look deep into your Inner Child eyes and tell them you love them and ask them to forgive you for not acknowledging them sooner. Reassure them that you are never going to abandon them or reject them again. Ask them to trust you. I placed a rose quartz crystal on my photograph, which I keep on my desk so I can daily acknowledge my Inner Child.

If like me you had no photographs of yourself when you were a child, ask older relatives if they have any of you. The photograph I use is one my sister gave me. She kindly had copies made of the original, which my mother had given to her. The photograph is of my sister, brother and me.

If you have more than one photograph carry one with you in your purse, wallet, inside your mobile phone cover, anywhere where you will come into contact with it during the day.

Activity Three

There are some excellent CDs of guided meditations, I use them frequently and will often play them whilst I fall asleep. They work subliminally with the subconscious mind, so it is not detrimental to their effectiveness when you fall asleep. There are others guided meditations that require you to take a more active role, as you interact with your Inner Child through imagery. The Journey by Brandon Bays is an excellent guided mediation, which is discussed in more detail in Part Four.

Activity Four

This is not a one off, activity. It needs to become part of your being; something that becomes second nature; talking to your Inner Child throughout the day it is not as crazy as it sounds. Think for a moment how many times do you have a conversation with yourself? You discuss things in your head. You hear yourself asking a question "Should I empty the kitchen bin now or leave it until after dinner when there may be more rubbish", "Should I put the washing out to dry or use the tumble dryer?" We all experience, this inner dialogue. In your mind talk to your Inner Child, praise them when you accomplish something, congratulate them, use encouraging words, tell them how good they are doing. Praise them; chances are they received very little praise when they were young.

Activity Five

Make a list of all the people associated with your past that you are angry with.
The list could include the abuser, your parents, relatives, those who didn't believe you when you told them what had happened, those who called you a liar, those who blamed you, anyone who didn't protect you. You have a right to be angry about being sexually abused. No one has the right to sexually abuse you. No one. And no one can take away that right for you to become angry.

Anger—Friend or Foe

It is said, that of all the emotions that will surface on your road to recovery anger will be the most frightening emotion you will have to deal with. Expressing anger allows you to experience a very strong emotion, which is essential for those who have become emotionally detached from their true self or Inner Child. Anger can be a very strong component in your recovery as it is empowering. It allows you to express yourself whilst diminishing the impact of fear that has governed your life for so long. The majority of adults with a history of child sexual abuse identified that fear was engrained in them.

When I attempted to write my list of those who I felt anger towards, I genuinely couldn't truthfully say that I felt anger towards anyone. Although I do question how I would respond if I discovered that one of my own daughters had been subjected to sexual abuse. Would I be passive, or would I want to physically attack the perpetrator? You often feel the injustice or plight of others more intensively than how you regard your own injustice. According to books I have read regarding connection to the Inner Child, anger management was considered essential in the quest to recover from the childhood sexual abuse.

One author said if you could not express anger it indicated that you are emotionally shut down and needed the assistance of a qualified psychotherapist to enable you to recover, which was not an option for me.

Even though I felt I was advancing on my healing journey the issue of anger provoked doubts; was I deluding myself, was the psychotherapist, right? I had carried out some of the anger activities, but I didn't experience any great relief, especially from the activities, which involved a physical reaction such as hitting and kicking. I then had a revelation regarding myself. I recalled that as a child, anger was not something I displayed. True, I lived in a house where anger was a common occurrence but my response to anger was feelings of fear and hurt.

Definition of Anger

A strong feeling of frustration, displeasure or hostility; the feeling of wanting to hurt another person

Could it be that I cannot express anger for the fear of hurting others like other people's anger had hurt me? I am not sure, but one thing I am sure of is that one pill does not cure all in our quest for recovery. I can become annoyed at things or frustrated when the phone rings and it's someone cold calling and I am in the middle of a meal. Or frustrated when I am trying to make an appointment or talk to the bank, and I am sixth in line. I get extremely annoyed when I hear or read of injustice towards others especially children and animals.

So, when does being annoyed or frustrated become anger? The fact that I was able to assess my response to anger was a benchmark that I was in touch with my true self or Inner Child. I no longer felt that I needed to conform to other people's opinion as law. I had learnt to value my own opinion and believe it is credible.

Another reason why I don't feel that displaying anger was essential to my recovery relates to the Reiki healing I received and was initiated into. The Reiki precepts that I practice states "For today I will not be angry".

It is impossible to cover anger in any depth other than to touch the surface of this emotive subject.

You know yourself if anger management is an area that you need to research in more detail. For some the releasing of anger is a major breakthrough in the recovery process. If you don't acknowledge the inner anger the consequences are that it can cause you both physical and emotional problems. Suppressing your anger can prevent you from moving forward in your recovery, by continuing to make you feel both guilty and ashamed.

If you fall into this category you need to take active measures to deal with the past and move forward. Anger management is one of the tools, which will enable you to achieve that release of the past and let go. Let's consider some of the activities available to release your suppressed anger. They fall into four different techniques, visualising, verbalising, writing and physical releasing. There will be one technique that works best for you, for example if you find the activities that are more of a violent nature feel uncomfortable with you, you may prefer to work on the writing activity to release your anger. Or try visualising a physical activity. There is no right or wrong way of releasing anger. It is what works for you.

Releasing Anger Activities

Physical Exercises

Prior to the activity calm your mind by closing your eyes and taking some deep breaths. Try and visualise the person that you want to vent your anger at. Another option is to place a photograph of that person near you, whilst carrying out the physical exercise.

Activities of a physical nature are better carried out when you won't feel inhibited by others. Try and find a time where you can be on your own and not likely to have any disturbances.

- Find a bat or tennis racket or any device that you can use to lash out, a stick, or a child's plastic sword would also work.
- Take a pillow and place it on the floor, kneel down and with some power strike the pillow. Ideally verbally express your anger with words, it could be name calling, or telling them how their actions have affected your life. Do this several times until you feel some emotion within yourself as you release this pent-up anger in a positive way.
- With your feet kick a pillow or a soft object. Kick a ball against a wall.
- Stamp on egg cartons or tin cans. Write the name of the abuser on a piece of paper and place on the floor then jump on the paper, whilst verbally expressing your anger.
- Destroy any photographs that evoke painful memories by tearing them into shreds. Again, verbally using words e.g. Get out of my Life, You are scum, try and speak from the depth of your heart don't be too surprised if your language is not for the ears of children, as you use words that are not typical of your vocabulary.
- Bury your head in a pillow and scream as loud as you can. Scream in the shower, scream in the car; make sure windows are closed and you have the radio turned on, or you may attract attention that you could do without.
- Go to a sport event and scream and shout at the

appropriate time, but mentally focus on the person you are angry with. This is very powerful way of releasing tension and anger. Scream anywhere when you are on your own home alone or out in nature where no one can hear you.

Writing activities

This is a good activity to start the process of releasing your anger. It will suit those of you who prefer a non-physical approach. It could also prove to be a stepping- stone, preparing you at a later date to practice the physical exercises. Do not restrict or censor what comes into your mind—write from your heart.

The purpose of the letters is to give you the opportunity to express your suppressed anger. When you have completed the letter, you can either tear it up or set fire to it, both are symbolic. I wrote several letters to my mother over the years but there was no visible theme of anger in the letters as I had successfully dealt with the anger issue towards both her and those who I felt had not protected me as a child.

Dear Mother

I am sorry to learn that you have been ill and needed to go in hospital. I received a voice message from a lady called Judith who I believe you met whilst in hospital. The message said that you wanted me to ring you.

I am sorry this is not possible as I made a calculated decision on the 19th, September 2012 when you slammed the phone down on me after calling me a dirty bitch AGAIN to completely detach from you.

A few years ago, you wrote me a letter, which I still have that said that you would never call me a DIRTY BITCH again and that it was unforgivable what you called me and that you can understand if I didn't want to have anything to do with you again. So hopefully you will understand my decision.

There are lots of things I could say but what would that achieve? I clearly remember you saying that you should never have had children and that my family were shite. Words are powerful weapons and cause so much hurt. I have had to live with the shame of being sexually abused and your words reinforced that shame and pain. But not anymore, I made a promise to myself that I will not allow you to hurt me again. I am NOT a dirty bitch. I was only a child who had a mother who didn't care.

I will continue to pray for you daily as I have always done. I truly do feel sorry for you as I see you as a very bitter, angry, hurting old lady who over the years has alienated her family and now finds herself alone.

Love and Prayers

I never sent the letter I believe it would not have achieved anything positive other than confirm to my mother that she was right that I was the one who was in the wrong. It did however give me a sense of control and helped me emotionally detach further from her.

Before you commence writing set some time aside and ensure that you will not be disturbed. If possible, have a photograph of either yourself as a child or a family photograph. An object that has links to your childhood or the time when the abuse took place would also be useful. Close your eyes and take some deep breaths. Now start to write stating why you are angry with the person. Don't ask questions enquiring why did you or how did you. Focus on statements like 'I am angry with you because you stole my childhood', 'I am angry at you because you knew what was going on and ignored it'. You will be surprised at once you start writing how the words just flow. You may want to write to several individuals who were involved; the abuser, parents, siblings, relatives anyone who had any involvement in the abuse. You may decide to keep the letters with a view of eventually sending them. They could act as a draft for you to modify and send out. Remember the purpose of these activities is to benefit you by encouraging you to connect to your feelings with the aim of letting go of the past moving forward.

Imagination Therapy Exercises

Imagining a situation where you become angry with the abuser or other individuals who didn't believe you, or protect you, may be the best method to adopt in preference to the physical anger release activities.

Prepare a room with two chairs facing each other. Sit in one of the chairs and imagine the person you are angry with is sitting in the chair opposite you. Take several deep breaths and hold a picture of the individual in your mind then vent all your suppressed anger at the person. Tell them exactly how you feel towards them.

Again, language you may not choose to use may surface, don't hold back just let it flow and become aware of how your body feels as you release the anger. If possible, record your words so you can reconnect with feelings of control you implemented over the abuser or person that you are angry with.

All of the above techniques are not a one size fits all quick fix solution. You may need to frequently practise them until the anger you previously felt towards them has been released. How will you know this has been achieved? You will experience an inner peace when the abuse comes into your mind, or you are involved in a conversation or exposed to some media coverage of sexual abuse. You will no longer experience the physical response with muscle tightening, especially in the shoulders and jaw area, feeling agitated, altered breathing pattern or an increase in heart rate.

The road to freedom is through the doorway of forgiveness—
Louise Hay

Forgiveness

So where do you sit with forgiveness? I cannot tell you what to do, but I do know it is an important issue on your healing journey, which you will need to address if you are to move on. By forgiving you are releasing resentment and anger. Forgiveness comes from your heart, and anger is the result of a hurting heart.

If you are struggling with forgiveness towards those that hurt you, whether it be physically or emotionally don't think that by forgiving them you are saying that their actions towards you are now acceptable; that is far from the truth. You are doing this for you, and **you** only. If you cannot learn to forgive you will always remain the victim. Forgiveness is a gift to you. Imagine being locked up in a prison cell and holding the key in your hand. When you use the key to open the cell door you are free; that is what forgiveness is. But only you can open the door, only you hold the key.

Forgiveness has not been a major issue for me. By accepting that my mother is incapable of fulfilling her role as a mother due to the possibility of her suffering with NPD, she therefore cannot be accountable for her behaviour towards me. However, this is questionable by some leading experts in NPD who say that through working with clients with NPD that they are fully aware of the consequence of their action towards others. They just cannot see why they should do things differently.

My mother doesn't see she has done anything wrong. Therefore, the need to forgive was to help me not her. Many believe that forgiveness should only be offered when the person involved is sorry for their actions and asks for forgiveness. By not forgiving I would still be influenced by her. Something I am no longer prepared for her to do.

My mother had robbed me of so much through her behaviour towards me denying me the opportunity to discover the real me and to meet my own needs. Once I let my mother go, I became aware of my true essence. It was then my own healing commenced. If I had not been able to forgive, I would have remained a victim allowing the past to control my future.

I give myself the gift of freedom from the past, and move with joy into the now—Louise Hay

There is a saying "I will forgive but never forget", for too many years I tried to forget about my past, I knew it had happened, but I tried to forget the trauma it had caused me by blocking out any association with child sexual abuse. I did not pretend it had not happened, I simply refused to engage with any memories of the abuse. It remained a festering wound that was calling for my attention. It needed to be opened cleaned and filled with love for myself. Through healing I have embraced the past and accepted what had taken place. I had been a victim too long. I believe you can forgive without forgetting.

Whilst I would not have chosen my parents, they have been my greatest teachers and have made me the person I am today. From that perspective good can come out of every situation if you focus on the positive not the negative. It is said that all suffering is caused by wanting things to be different. By accepting the past can never be changed and memories can never be erased, you can choose to view the past differently, if you don't the consequences are it will bind you to the past and prevent you from letting go and moving on.

We had no choice regarding the past, but we do have a choice regarding the future.

I have also used the fact that I have truly forgiven my parents as a benchmark of my progress of being free of the past.

I have been asked if I have forgiven the uncle involved with the sexual abuse. I can verbally forgive him, but I question if he was ever sorry about his behaviour towards me. It is possible that I wasn't the only child he abused and bullied. Being entirely honest I don't know if I could look him in the eye and say, 'I forgive you' and truly mean it. This reluctance to forgive their predators is not unusual for child sexual abuse victims; it is beneficial to their own healing to assert blame and anger towards them.

I do believe that there is a higher source which gives us strength to accomplish things we would never think we are capable of achieving. I feel that it doesn't just work in physical achievements but in issues relating to the heart and emotions such as forgiveness.

My mother sent me a letter in July 2016, the background to the letter was that she had fallen and been taken into hospital for surgery for a dislocated hip. Whilst in hospital she was befriended by a lady who rang me to say my mother wanted to see me. I shared with her why I no longer have any contact with my mother, but if she wanted to get in touch again, she could write to me.

A few weeks later a note arrived from her.

Dear Lynne

I'm writing to ask you to forgive me for the hurt I've caused you in the past. I'm so sorry I do miss you. I've lost my dog - it broke my heart; I wish you and your family health and happiness in the future. I send you all my love.

Mum.

After much soul searching, I sent her the following:

Dear Mum

I am sorry to learn that you are far from well and things are challenging for you at the moment.

Regarding forgiveness forgiving you has never been a problem. I have never been a person who has held a grudge or looked for revenge. My problem is that whilst I do forgive you, please believe me, however, that I am afraid that you will hurt me again.

Over the years you have said you were sorry three times for the cruel things you have called me. You even wrote to me several years ago and promised you would never call me a dirty bitch again. I have kept that letter.

It is good that you have Christian people in your life now, who are helping and supporting you. I have never stopped praying for you mum, which I hope you will find reassuring.

Regarding Buster sometimes you have to love someone enough to let them go. You must find comfort knowing he is with a family who can take him for walks and care for all his needs.

I will pass on your love to the rest of the family

Love and Prayers

Lynne

My mother never replied to my letter, part of me was glad she didn't, but, more disturbingly, I became aware that there was a part of me, which needed her to confirm the rejection. I was so used to being rejected it felt the norm; in a weird way I felt

159

secure.

I will never know if my mother is truly sorry for her actions towards me. There is a saying, "A leopard can never change its spots". She had said sorry before, but as time has demonstrated her attitude towards me didn't reflect her sincerity. I then questioned if it would make any difference if she were genuinely sorry, it certainly could never change the course of my childhood.

It did however make me more determined to let go of any remaining negative memories associated with my mother, as the negativity served as a chain to the past. I read in one of my daily reading books that when circus elephants are young and unaware of their strength, they are bound by a chain to a stake to limit their mobility. Later when they are fully grown and have the strength to break that chain, they are still bound, because they accept this limitation as permanent. But it is not the chain that keeps them bound it is the memory. Painful negative childhood memories keep us chained to the past and the only way to truly be free is to forgive those you hold responsible, to stop the past dictating your future.

It is now safe for me to forgive all my childhood traumas. I am free—Louise Hay

Change your Thoughts Change your Life

I work closely with the Law of Attraction, which is discussed in more detail in Part Four. It is by working with the Law of Attraction daily that I am able attract positive thought patterns regarding the past. The basic new age philosophy is that you attract back what you personally give out. Like attracts like. By focusing on positive or negative thoughts a person brings positive and negative experiences into their lives. It is based on the belief that people are made of pure energy and that energy attracts like energy. If this is resonating with you there is a wealth of material on the Law of Attraction on the Internet. Rhonda Byrne, a modern pioneer of the old age philosophy, has produced books including The Secret, which was also made into a short documentary film, The Power, The Magic, and the Hero.

There are many other books and articles on the Internet, which will give you in depth information on this philosophy and how you can involve aspects of it in your daily life. There have been several occasions when the Law of Attraction has manifested in my life. I have used vision boards to attract the desired outcomes with excellent results. In fact, the thought and desire to write this book first went on a vision board.

In conjunction with The Law of Attraction and the need to break free from the negativity associated with the past, I embarked upon a letter writing quest, which allowed me to divert the negativity surrounding my childhood to a positive one by changing the energy I associated with it. It allowed me for the first time to put my account of the situation forward, which I had never had the opportunity to do before.

Setting the Records Straight

Throughout life we all experience situations when we wish we could rewrite the script and avoid the consequence that resulted from our actions. Think for a moment—are there some individuals that due to circumstances beyond your control you have hurt, let down or failed? Writing letters to them is very therapeutic, it allows you to bring a sense of closure to the situation by attempting to give your own account of the situation and making them consider the reason for your actions.

The following letters are to people associated with my childhood who I feel through circumstances beyond my control I have either hurt, failed or let down. I want to ask for their forgiveness. I have no way of contacting these individuals to verbally tell them why I acted the way I did. Whilst working with my Inner Child I discovered that like so many other issues relating to my childhood these negative feelings had been locked deep within my sub conscious mind and my Inner Child needed to have the opportunity to present the reasons for her behaviour.

After I had wrote the letters, I imagined the person concerned was with me as I read the letter to them.

Auntie Delia

You were a very special person in my life. I used to pretend that you were my mother because you were always kind to me. You introduced me to reading books. We used to go to the library on a Saturday afternoon where you would get me a book every week on your ticket. I loved going back to your house and reading my book. You gave me jewellery that you didn't want any more. You took me to the races and to watch motorbike scrambling. You once took me on holiday and bought me a pale blue jumper.

I never got the opportunity to say thank you. Years later you told my mother that you were disappointed that I didn't invite you to my wedding after all you had done for me. I can understand why you felt that way towards me.

Two things happened which prevented me from coming to see you, which I never shared with you.

There was an occasion when you too didn't believe me. Do you remember when you took me on holiday and Uncle G came to visit us for the day? When he was going home, we went to the bus station with him. As he was leaving, I started to cry. You asked why, I said that I felt sorry for Uncle G not being able to stay with us and having to go home when we were having such a lovely time.

You didn't believe me. You said I was crying because he hadn't given me the money he had promised and that was the reason I was crying.

I tried to explain it wasn't the money, but you insisted that it was all about the money. I was upset that you didn't believe me. It could have been because you didn't like the fact that I showed affection towards Uncle G. I know you loved me like the daughter you never had, and I was special to you.

The other reason that I stopped coming involved Uncle G again. There was an occasion when you had hurt your back and had to have complete bed rest. I stayed upstairs with you for most of the afternoon but went downstairs to help Uncle G make the tea. I can even remember it was a salad and you always added mint sauce to the lettuce. It was whilst preparing the salad that Uncle G suddenly grabbed hold of me and pushed me against the wall and started to grab my breasts. I screamed and he let me go but then tried to stop me coming upstairs to you. He kept hold of my wrist until I calmed down. He begged me not to tell you. When I eventually came back upstairs you asked me why I had screamed, I told you a lie. I said that Uncle G had said there was a mouse watching me.

How could I have told you the truth? Would you have believed me? You didn't believe me about the crying when Uncle G went home. So that is the reason why I stopped coming to see you. I never told anyone about Uncle G; I kept it a secret. Although he didn't really physically hurt me, emotionally it caused me so much pain. I missed you so much. Saturdays were never the same. I always felt that there was something missing. I really loved you.

I am so sorry that I hurt you; please forgive me. I had to stay away as I couldn't go through the experience again of not being believed. This happened when I told Auntie Alice about Frank and the sexual abuse that he was subjecting me to. You were not aware of this. No one knew except Auntie Alice and my mother who did believe me but allowed it to happen. Hope this helps you to understand the reasons for my actions and why I didn't invite you to my wedding.

School Teacher

I am still so grateful to you for being so kind to me at school and helping me in more ways than I think you realise. You passed me as being competent for a guide badge, even though I could not do the poses as I constantly needed to stop, as my bra was held together with safety pins that kept opening and sticking into me.

On another occasion you told me that you had put

my name forward to go to Camp School although I hadn't been initially selected but another pupil had broken her leg and was unable to go. You would also ask me to go to the shop for you at lunchtime. You seemed to be aware that I was very unhappy and was struggling not with schoolwork but with the home situation. This was probably due to your husband being an insurance agent and calling at our house to collect money from my mother.

I know that there was an occasion, which involved my mother when you didn't believe me. I had come to school late as my mother had lost her temper and smashed several items in the house including a glass panel in a door. She had vented her anger at my brother and me and to avoid more beatings we had both gone to school upset and late.

You were not my form teacher, but I was on the corridor waiting to go into to a lesson when you passed by. I ended up explaining why I was late.

That night your husband called at our home on the pretext that he needed to discuss a new contract or policy. By this time my mother had calmed down and everything appeared normal. I remember my mother didn't invite him into the house, as there was quite a lot of damage where she had thrown things. The broken window in the door was visible but I don't think your husband saw it. I remember being so worried that he would say something relating to me being upset at school, thankfully he didn't. But after that, things changed at school. You no longer would smile at me or ask me to go to the shops for you. You distanced yourself from me, which I felt was a direct result of your husband visiting us that night.

I just need you to know that I wasn't telling lies or exaggerating. I also want to thank you for giving me

165

the hope and encouragement to work hard with my school studies.

Male School Teacher

I want the opportunity to explain why I let you down and failed to attend night school that you had organised for me. As you know although I had good grades my mother would not let me stay on at school to do my O levels despite several teachers, you included writing on my report card things like "It is a great shame that Lynne is unable to stay on at school and do what she wants to do", "Lynne is a very capable student who always works hard"

If you remember I had to leave the A stream and go into a class with other pupils who were also not staying on at school. It was a pilot scheme, which involved very little academic subjects, only basic English and Maths. The rest of the curriculum focused on sports and vocational training. You kindly arranged for me to attend the local college to do English and Maths O levels after school.

I am sorry that I didn't attend; I could tell by your demeanour that you were disappointed when I told you I hadn't attended. What I failed to tell you at the time were the reason why, as it may have been seen as a criticism.

You only gave me verbal instructions as to where to go, you said the room number for English language and the room number would be on a list in the entrance hall. I did go there on the first night—I was so nervous.

I couldn't find a list with the room numbers. There were lots of other older students around, but I lacked the confidence to ask any of them. I also noticed that they all had files and bags, which I presumed had writing material in and paper. I had not considered that I needed to bring my own writing paper and pens. I then became so anxious that I just left the college feeling a failure for letting you down. It was just too much for me to do. I lacked both confidence and self-esteem.

Thank you for believing in me and seeing that I had potential to achieve. I eventually did my nurse training and obtained a degree in health studies and then went on to become a college lecturer with a teaching qualification. I am now a holistic practitioner and teacher. You gave me the motivation to succeed because you saw something in me that many had failed to recognise. Thank you.

Auntie Alice

You were very kind to me. I used to enjoy our special walks together. I inherited your fear of thunderstorms and I remember you making me go under the table during a thunderstorm and taking out any metal clips I had in my hair. I suppose to a certain degree I can understand why you reacted the way you did when I told you what Uncle Frank was doing. You said I was telling lies and that he loved me and would never hurt me. You were wrong and by telling him what I had told you he was annoyed at me. So, it continued to happen when he used to babysit for my mother on a Friday night. When my mother eventually confronted him and stopped him from coming, I was not allowed to come to your house.

Months later someone told my mother that you were very poorly. I didn't dare come and see you, so I made you some flower essences. I collected rose

167

petals and put them in a bottle with spring water. I came to your house rang the doorbell and then ran away. The next day I came back, and the bottle was still on the doorstep.

I then heard that you had died in hospital. I was upset that you did not believe me, but I never attributed any blame to you. It's strange that you did not believe me, but my mother did. I do not need to ask you to forgive me as I was only a little girl, but I want to tell you I loved you. I do know you loved me too.

The letters were a great healing tool, they allowed me to express and release some deep-rooted concerns that I had carried for so long. It concerned me that I had failed these individuals who had showed me love and encouragement. Once I had addressed my concerns and read the letters several times, I was convinced that I could not have acted any differently. I had to constantly remember that I was only a child when the incidents happened, and the main driving force was one of survival. The letter that brought me the greatest release was to my own Inner Child, who had carried all the hurt and guilt of my childhood:

Hello Poppet

I am so sorry that I have ignored you all these years. I didn't do it to hurt you; I simply didn't know you were there. I now know I treated you like the others; never listening to you, never considering your needs, never allowing you to play and be a child, never encouraging you to laugh and to feel secure and loved, without fear of being punished for being you—a gentle, caring, frightened little girl. Please forgive me, your adult self, for rejecting you sweetheart. Yes, I am talking to you little Lynne. I know you are not used to hearing words of affection directed at you. You were fed on negative words, "Dirty Bitch", "Lazy Bitch" and starved of positive words, never hearing words of encouragement, words of love, words of appreciation. You were so brave, so strong. The harder you tried to be loved the more you felt the pain of rejection.

So, you became invisible, hiding away having no voice. I understand why it is so hard for you to trust someone and why you feel safer in your hellish hole. I am asking you to forgive me for the past.

I want to help you to give you back some of the things that you were denied. I want to fill your world with happiness and love if you will let me? I promise to listen to you and never leave you all alone again.

Thank you for being you, thank you for enduring the past, which has made me who I am today, your adult self.

I love you.

> **The way ahead is clear and free**
> **I give myself permission to move**
> **out of the past with gratitude,**
> **and into a joyous day**—Louise Hay

I encourage you to consider delving into your past to discover if there are people dead or alive who hold emotional ties over you. Writing letters to them is a constructive way of expressing your inner thoughts and releasing any negativity that is associated with them.

In Part Four you will discover other therapies that suggest

how to communicate and develop a deeper relationship with your Inner Child.

Part Four

Healing Therapies

There are several therapies available that will help you on your healing journey. I have selected therapies that have been the most instrumental in my own personal healing. Whilst the majority of the therapies I used have no or very little substantial scientific research to promote their credibility I do not feel that in any way does it devalue the amazing effect they had on my life. I am sure there will be some therapies that are more appealing to you than others. We are all unique individuals; one size doesn't necessarily fit all as I mentioned previously.

The common denominator is they are all self-healing therapies, which you can explore with in the privacy of your own home. The only exception is Reiki. I recommend that the initial Reiki treatment, be carried out by a Reiki practitioner. You may at some point decide that you want to be attuned to the Reiki energy which will enable you to do daily self-healing.

I don't believe that any one of the therapies were more beneficial than the others it was the whole package of therapies that collectively produced the positive result. It is the same philosophy when working with herbs, one herb in isolation is therapeutic but a synergy of herbs working in harmony with each other can produce even more amazing results. I think this is true with the therapies that I chose to help me on my healing journey. Collectively they worked in a truly holistic way.

The Twelve Therapies

1 – Reiki
2 – Sound Massage
3 – Crystal Healing
4 – Angel therapy
5 – Mirror Work—Louise Hay

6 – The Healing Codes
7 – Donna Eden Energy Workouts
8 – Ho'oponopno Hawaiian healing therapy
9 – Flower Essences
10 – Emotional Freedom Tapping
11 – Law of Attraction
12 – The Journey by Brandon Bays

Most of the therapies share the same principle and work in conjunction with each other, the majority fall under the category of energy medicine.

Another approach to health is the revelation that cells within our bodies hold memories some of which are destructive, (referred to as destructive cellular memories), which are the cause of both physical and emotional health problems. All the therapies that I selected are intertwined within the philosophy of energy medicine and cellular memories.

Energy Medicine

There is a new frontier in healing that does not involve the use of pharmaceutical drugs or conventional medical treatments. In 1905 Albert Einstein stated that everything is energy, and everything boils down to energy—there is nothing that is not energy. It is the life force. When it is present you are alive and when you do not have life force you are pronounced physically dead. It is energy that dictates the way your body functions, directing your immune system and organs. These energies have amazing capabilities, far smarter than your intelligence at keeping you healthy, by maintaining balance and initiating inner healing strategies that you are not aware of when you become unwell.

Energy is all around us in different wavelengths and frequencies, from energies with short wavelengths like cosmic radiation and x-rays to long wavelengths such as radio waves and infrared waves.

Our voice also releases sound waves, which cause movement in the air around us and when we think, our brains release wavelengths of energy to. All our health problems originate from a destructive energy frequency.

Energy medicine is used to treat illness, relieve pain, stimulate the immune system response, reduce stress levels, improve memory and generally promote wellbeing. Throughout history healers have been defined as someone who facilitates healing in another, by tapping into and empowering one's own healing capacity in that individual.

The greatest scientists of our time have also promoted the concept of energy. According to Richard Gerber MD "The ultimate approach to healing will be to remove the abnormalities at the subtle-energy level which lead to the manifestation of illness in the first place". Many Noble Prize winners also state that the root of all health problems is an energy issue within the body. This emerging approach to health is both ancient and modern. According to Albert Szent-Gyorgyi, Nobel Laureate in medicine, "In every culture and in every tradition before ours, healing was accomplished by moving energy".

There is a shared belief amongst many, myself, included, that someday we are going to invent a way of fixing the energy problem that underlines every health issue presented and when this happens the concepts of health will change forever. Dr Mehmet Oz, also known as "America's Doctor," declared on Oprah Winfrey's show and in his bestselling book, "YOU" that "Energy medicine is a legitimate and effective modality and the next big frontier in medicine".

The purpose of energy therapies can be broadly defined as the healing of mental or physical disorders by rebalancing the energy fields in the human body, or by drawing upon spiritual energies such as Reiki and self-healing. Some energy therapies include emotional detoxification, to release trauma stored in the memory of the cells.

Just as there are many different types of medicine available from the pharmaceutical companies, there are different types of energy medicine. Many have ancient healing traditions such as Yoga, Qi Gong, Shiatsu, Reiki and Acupuncture, whilst others such as Healing Touch, Therapeutic Touch, Emotional Freedom Tapping and Kinesiology have evolved within the last century.

Energy medicine can be complimentary to orthodox medicine or a complete system for self-care and self-help. It addresses physical illness along with emotional or mental health. Energy medicine adopts a truly holistic approach by addressing issues related to mind, body and spirit. In an attempt to relate to the concepts of energy medicine it is helpful to be aware of the energy that is associated with the physical body and beyond.

The Meridians

As the arteries transport blood around the body, the meridians are the body's energy pathways. The fourteen main meridians carry a flow of energy that adjusts metabolism and energises every organ and the eleven physiological systems in the body. These pathways exist in the subtle body being the invisible field that surrounds and permeates the physical body. The meridians were a source of survival in ancient civilisations. Detecting the energy fields allowed ancient ancestors to detect the properties of plants, nutritious or poisonous. They were so attuned to energy that they were able to detect the approach of predators, whilst being able to sense when the energy of others was out of balance. The manuscripts from ancient cultures contain teaching material on how to balance the body's energy fields and keep the population of the time healthy.

The Chinese documented a system of working with energy pathways focusing on acupuncture, which is still being practiced today. It is instrumental in promoting health and fighting diseases associated with twenty-first century living.

Acupressure Points

Acupressure is a healing art that is both safe and holistic. It was developed in China, over five thousand, years ago. The technique works on charted meridian pathways. Pressure is exerted, using the thumb or fingers to press key points where energy pools. Both acupressure and acupuncture use the same points and meridians, acupuncture uses needles whilst acupressure uses the fingers. Tuning forks also work on the meridians; the tuning fork is activated by hitting it against an implement that causes it to vibrate and emit a frequency. This is then placed on the body in relation to the meridian or energy pathways that correspond to the organ or system that needs re-balancing.

Acupressure is used for physical pain and emotional pain along with trauma and addictions. It boosts the immune system and is used for stress and relaxation.

The Aura

The aura is sometimes referred to as the Biofield, a multi layered protective energy field that extends around the entire body. It varies from each individual, as an array of changing spectrum of colours. It interacts with the physical body and is influenced by your emotions and atmosphere that you are experiencing. There are some practitioners who can see the aura of an individual and interpret and redefine the aura. Many believe that illness and disease are initially structured with the aura, as the body and aura work in conjunction with each other, the imbalance in the aura if not rectified results in disease within the physical body.

Cellular Memories

Before explaining individual therapies that are based on releasing cellular memories to promote emotional healing, we need to explore the theory involved and gain understanding of the philosophy.

According to the Science of Cellular Healing, the lining of your stomach regenerates itself, every two to three days, and every two days we literally see with brand new eyes as the cells in your eyes are renewed. Your liver cells renew completely every six to seven weeks, amazing facts. Consider when you have a suntan the reason why it fades in two or three weeks is due to the cells in our skin being replaced with new ones.

It is attributed to cells replications, the cell divides, and the new cell takes on the old cell's memory or information. If the process of cell replication was that simple liver cancer and other degenerative diseases would not exist as in the case of the liver, the cells are completely renewed in six to seven days. The pioneering work of M.D. Deepak Chopra explains that the cell memory is carried on and passed on to each new generation of cells. In the case of cancer, the new cells pass on the degenerative cancer message through cell memory.

Once this cell memory is released the cell is given the message to return to its normal healthy state, this explains spontaneous healing when the body, despite all odds, is fully healed overnight.

With this revelation it questions why our cells ever become diseased. Dr Candace Pert an accredited molecular biologist and author of the book Molecules of Emotions claims to have the answer to this mystery. Her studies revealed that repressed emotions have a direct effect on our cells. In each cell there is a cell receptor site. In a simplified account the cell receptors are keyholes in each cell that allows the brain to communicate with each other on how to stay healthy and in a state of homeostasis. The brain produces chemical messengers called neuropeptides, which travel through the body. They are the keys that fit into the cell receptors. This is the way the mind and the body communicate.

If the body experiences prolonged intense emotions such as grief, stress, depression, fear, anxiety or anger the body becomes overpowered with chemical neuropeptides, which block the cell receptor sites effectively blocking the cells from communicating with each other. The consequence of this prolonged heightened emotional state results in the likelihood of disease manifesting in the part of the body where there are blocked cell receptors and no communication between the cells.

This causes blocked emotions to get locked into our bodies at a cellular level. Science has now discovered there is a correlation between our health and suppressed emotions. The more an individual, expresses emotions the healthier that individual is. It is estimated that 98 per cent of all disease is linked to cellular memories. Both acute and chronic diseases are prevalent along with a suppressed immune system.

According to Dr John Sarno, professor of, medicine New York University, "Our best hope for healing incurable illnesses and disease in the future might well lie in finding a way to heal destructive cellular memories. If you can heal that cellular memory, then the illness, disease or chronic pain is very likely to heal".

Whilst science and orthodox medicine have this knowledge, they have not yet found a repeatable effective method for unblocking the cell receptors site that are creating disease.

This is where therapies such as the Healing Code and Brandon Bays therapy, The Journey, have their roots and shared philosophy along with other healing modalities such as Reiki, Emotional Freedom Tapping, Flower Essence and Sound Massage.

Let's now consider some of the therapies whose core principle is energy.

Reiki

Reiki was the first of the energy therapies that I experienced on my healing journey. I never made a conscious decision to become involved in Reiki due to my mother's belief in fortune telling and tarot cards, plus the influence of church doctrines, which taught that Reiki was linked to the occult. I distanced myself from any kind of association with Reiki.

I now believe that Reiki found me as the saying goes. I was studying for a Diploma in Holistic Therapies. One particular class, much to my disgust I hasten to add, involved a guest speaker on Reiki. I was so anti Reiki I told another student if I had known the session was about Reiki I would not have come. We sat in two semi circles around a massage bed. I strategically placed myself on the back row to distance myself. Following the theory of Reiki, the speaker asked for a volunteer to receive a treatment; there were several volunteers.

Once the Reiki Master had performed the healing and the student had given feedback, stating that she experienced a tingling sensation and felt the heat of the healer's hands, the Reiki Master looked straight at me and asked me to come and carry out healing on the same student. Initially I declined but she became even more insistent, that she wanted me to do it despite several other students volunteering. Reluctantly I came forward. She showed me where to place my hands over the student and how to rotate them near to the student's head. The Reiki Master closed her eyes and muttered something. I then placed my hands over the student as instructed, within probably twenty seconds the student said she could feel the energy coming from my hands.

Even more astounding was I too could feel a tingling sensation in my hands. I dismissed the sensation, telling myself that if you hold your hand out its obvious that you would experience a tingling sensation. At that point I certainly wasn't convinced. I now realise that not only was I both mentally and emotionally blocked, cellular memories, were influencing my resistance in becoming engaged in Reiki as I associated it with having links to my mother and her activities.

It was several months later that Reiki once again came into my life, this time through a client who had come to the clinic for a treatment. She was a Reiki Master and told me during her treatment that my throat chakra was blocked and I needed a Reiki healing to unblock the chakra. She explained that a blocked throat chakra indicates that I was not speaking my truth and my words were being suppressed causing me digestive and other health problems. I resisted and did nothing.

The next client that promoted Reiki was more forceful; she had been a Reiki Master for many years and had attuned many students to Reiki healing. During the treatment I told her why I resisted any involvement with Reiki. She told me that I was a healer and I had to stop resisting.

Following the recent encounters, it appeared that Reiki was everywhere, in magazines, clients of the clinic and even a friend was having regular Reiki sessions. I truly believe that my previous encounters with Reiki had started to open me up on a subconscious level. I read a book on Reiki and eventually had my first Reiki treatment with the Reiki Master to whom I had revealed my reluctance to become involved with Reiki.

Initially I decided to have three Reiki treatments in a relatively short period of time. Several months later I took my first Reiki attunement, and the following year I took my second attunement. I then started offering Reiki in the clinic. I believe Reiki was the catalyst for my healing. Following my experience with Reiki my life changed dramatically. I started my journey of recovery based on the principles of Reiki. I later became a Reiki Master.

What is Reiki?

It is often referred to as a hands-on healing technique delivered by human touch. The word Reiki translates to mean Universal Life Force. It is accessible to everyone through an attunement process, which is delivered by a Reiki Master. It is likened to the various frequencies, found when tuning into a radio, allowing you to access different radio stations. To access Reiki frequencies, you must connect to the correct frequency, which is only accessible when you have been attuned.

Reiki is everywhere, it is definitely not a religion, but it works in a spiritual vein. People of all religions and different cultures practice Reiki daily. It appears that there has been a decline in our spiritual awareness resulting in detachment from God, The Divine, The Almighty, The Great Spirit, The Higher Self, whatever you chose to call it has been neglected. However, the belief in a higher power is not a prerequisite for working with the Reiki energy. You do not need to believe in anything to access it other than wanting to work with it. It involves daily practice allowing the Reiki energy to work in you and through you. It is instrumental in promoting self-development, harmony and balance. I used to tell my students that once they were initiated into the Reiki energy their lives would never be the same again. It is like plugging an electric lawnmower into the mains to make it work as opposed to using a lawn mower that requires human exertion to make it work.

A misconception of Reiki is that the energy comes from the Reiki healer or person carrying out the Reiki session. This is not true; the person carrying out the treatment is nothing more than a channel or vessel for the Reiki energy to flow through. Many Reiki practitioners refuse to refer themselves as healers, acknowledging they are just instruments, to be used to bring this Universal Energy.

Often individuals seek Reiki in response to some medical problem or health concern. In many cases the dysfunction of the physical body is a consequence of emotional trauma, which is often the root cause of physical illness. Reiki works in a holistic way bringing harmony and balance within the body, mind and spirit. The essence of Reiki is pure love, something many of us were denied in our childhood.

Reiki Principles

There are Reiki principals that are integrated into daily living they are guidelines for promoting true happiness for those who practice them and make them a daily mantra. There are many different variations, but they all contain the same essence:

- Just for today I will let go of anger
- Just for today I will let go of worry
- Just for today I will give thanks for my many blessings
- Just for today I will do my work honestly
- Just for today I will be kind to my neighbour and every living thing.

You do not have to practice Reiki to embrace them into your life; they are guidelines for structuring your day. They will not only benefit you, they also benefit every living thing. If only more individuals would practise them the world would become a better place. This can be achieved by one life at a time. They should be repeated throughout the day, a good strategy is to write them out and place them anywhere that you will see them.

There are three degrees of Reiki that a Reiki practitioner can progress through.

First Degree

This is the starting point for anyone who desires to administer Reiki on themselves, members of their family and friends. Reiki energy is passed from the initiating Reiki Master, in a ceremonial manner to the Reiki student.

Second Degree

This involves being attuned to higher Reiki energy. This degree is known as Practitioner Level although many who are attuned have no desire to become Practitioners. During this attunement Sacred Symbols, along with Distance Healing are introduced, allowing healing to be sent anywhere around the world.

Third Degree

This is referred to as Master Level and is likened more to an apprenticeship and takes around a year to complete. Further symbols are introduced along with an initiation into higher Reiki energy.

Experiencing a Reiki Treatment

A Reiki treatment should be both a pleasure to give and receive.

The session normally lasts about one hour but do allow more time as the Reiki practitioner will allow you to share the experience with them but only if you wish. During a Reiki Treatment you are always in control; you do not have to share with the Reiki Practitioner anything you do not feel comfortable sharing. When I received my first Reiki Treatment, I did not divulge anything relating to my past childhood abuse. I was not ready to share with anyone as I explained. I am now convinced that Reiki instigated the healing I was subconsciously searching for. In a very loving and nurturing manner it started to break down the brick walls I had built around myself in an attempt to keep out the negativity, the pain and the shame associated with my childhood.

There are no two Reiki session that are ever identical so it is not possible to say exactly what will happen during the session.

The Reiki practitioner will place their hands strategically on or around twelve different places on your body. It is possible that you could experience heat tingling or even a coldness coming from their hands as the Reiki energy is being channelled into your body.

Some people report seeing bright coloured lights, which are associated with chakras and auras. The Reiki energy will work on whatever area is most damaged whether it is physical, mental or emotional.

The Chakras

Eastern cultures have long attributed wellbeing to the balancing chakras or vital energy centres within the body where life energy flows and is processed. There are seven vital energy centres. We cannot feel them or see them, they cannot be seen on an x-ray or MRI Scan. They are important in relation to our physical, mental and spiritual health.

In Sanskrit (an ancient Indian language) Chakra is defined as wheel or circle. Balanced chakras can be visualised as spinning wheels revolving in a clockwise direction at a particular frequency. When imbalanced, chakras may rotate in an anti-clockwise direction, which disrupts vital energy force. Chakras are linked to the endocrine system, which is instrumental in health. The endocrine system comprises of a number of ductless glands that produce hormones acting as chemical messages that are secreted into the blood stream, these then stimulate or inhibit physical processes. The position of the chakras corresponds to the position of the glands in the endocrine system and have effect on the function of the chakras.

It is said that there are 88,000 chakras in the body. There are seven principal chakras. The fact that there are seven major chakras conforms with natural rhythms, as there are seven colours of the rainbow, which are attributed to a specific chakra. There are also seven notes on a musical scale that are used in sound therapy to balance and realign.

Chakras are located vertically from the base of the spine to the top of the head. Life experiences such as illness, trauma, stress can cause imbalances resulting in the chakras becoming blocked and over-loaded. Imbalances produce a variety of health issues and disturbances to physical, mental and emotional health. Imbalances can be temporary but when prolonged they can cause chronic illness, disease and addictive patterns.

Root Chakra Red

Lower back pain, haemorrhoids, constipation, prostate problems, obesity, anorexia, varicose veins.

Sacral Chakra Orange

Impotence, frigidity, menstrual problems, urinary problems, lower back pain.

Solar Plexus Chakra Yellow

Digestive problems, food allergies and intolerances, diabetes, ulcers, liver problems, gallstones, adrenal imbalances, arthritis.

Heart Chakra Green or Pink

Heart problems, cardiovascular and circulation problems, hypertension, strokes, respiratory problems, upper back and shoulder problems, arthritis

Throat Chakra Blue

Thyroid problems, throat problems, laryngitis, dental problems, ear infections, spondylitis, stiff neck and shoulders.

Third Eye Chakra Purple

Headaches, sinusitis, brain tumours, visual problems, anxiety, depression.

Crown Chakra White

Musculoskeletal disorders, skin problems, chronic fatigue syndrome, hypersensitivity to light and sound.

Each chakra is associated with a specific colour as seen above. It is believed that the interaction between crystals and chakras will return the chakras into a healthy vibration, which can then infuse healing and balance to the part of the body the chakra represents.

In relation to the Inner Child the root chakra and the sacral chakras are often out of balance. Whilst working with clients to rebalance the chakras I have discovered that the heart chakra is also out of balance.

Sound Massage

My experience with sound in a healing context came about through receiving a sound massage treatment. It was recommended by one of my clients who had experienced a very powerful release in relation to blocked childhood emotions. As I was working with my Inner Child at the time, I was drawn to the revelation that we all carry emotional baggage that is locked in our cells and leads to problems with not only physical health issues but also with emotional issues. So powerful was my encounter with sound as a healing modality, I eventually became a qualified Sound Massage Practitioner. The training involved an intensive six-day course, my teacher was a wonderful inspirational soul. It remains the best course I have ever attended. To be enveloped in sound for almost a week was profound so much so that I found it hard to readjust to the explosion of noise I was exposed to at Malaga airport on my return.

What is Sound Massage?

Unlike Reiki you will be in the minority if you know anything about the healing virtues of Sound Massage. Whilst we are all aware of the role that music plays in our lives, we may not be aware of how we can use sound frequencies to eradicate blocked energy. Every day we are all affected by sound, it could be the sound of birds, children laughing, singing or music, along with sound of a more intense sensory effect such as loud music or noisy traffic. All sound generates an effect on our emotions, health and wellbeing.

The origin of Sound Massage is attributed to India. For over 5,000 years sound has been used in healing. By producing healing vibrations or frequencies the body is gently placed in a state of homeostasis and balance. The cells of the body are coerced into a state of harmony.

An image that will help you appreciate the philosophy behind sound massage is to visualise dropping a pebble into a pool of water, the pebble will cause circular waves of movement to generate outwards causing the entire area of water to actively move setting every molecule of the water into motion. The same philosophy takes place during a sound massage in our body, which consists of 70% water. Vibrations are carried through concentric waves massaging every 100 trillion cells in the body.

When the organs and tissues are free of blockages the sound waves travel around the body uninterrupted eventually exiting through our toes, fingertips and hair. Unfortunately, our bodies are usually not free of blockages as unresolved issues, stress and worries we encounter create blockages which result in both physical pain and emotional pain, as with arthritis along with the hardening of certain muscle groups and emotional pain trapped in the cells through destructive cellular memories.

In the early 1980s Peter Hess, a German engineer, became interested in the science of vibrational fields in the human body. He researched the effect of traditional music on both the body and the mind. Working with the people of Tibet and Nepal led to his work with the use of singing bowls and healing frequencies. His belief is that mankind is made through vibration. This is extended to include the vibration generated through all sound. The Holy mantras that are used in daily prayer are said to be the most important sounds in Tibet as they produce rhythmic vibrations through words. The belief that each individual has their own unique vibrational code and sound vibration is the key to health and harmony in both mind, body and spirit. According to Peter Hess the people of Nepal believe that a man who vibrates harmoniously is healthy. If discourse reigns within the body's cells, balance is lost, and illness is the consequence. However, if a sick man listens to harmonious sounds the body will rebalance, and health will pursue.

During a Sound Massage treatment singing bowls are placed either on your fully clothed body or very close to you within your aura. They are gently tapped with a mallet, which produces a beautiful humming echoing sound, which slowly diminishes. The bowls are played on various parts of the body including hands and feet. Different sizes of bowls are used, larger bowls are played on the lower parts of the body as they respond to lower frequencies, whilst smaller bowls are used in the higher regions of the body as they relate to higher frequencies.

This promotes balance, relaxation, inner strength and energy. The bowls work in a holistic manner working with pain, stress and anxiety. This is accomplished by deep relaxation, some people fall asleep very quickly, whilst some do reach the Theta stage associated with sleep patterns. This is where the mind completely surrenders allowing visions and dreams and sub conscious memories to be released. The cells of the body are gently brought back into a state of balance. Emotional blockages are removed. This results in an important aspect in our healing journey of letting go and moving on. Creativity and positivity are also increased.

Each sound massage session I personally encountered produced a different outcome, it was as if a layer of pain and grief was being taken away, it has been likened to the many skins of an onion.

I cannot truly remember how many sound massage treatments I had received before I encountered the most profound experience. In previous sessions I had always experienced a sense of intense relaxation, often seeing colours and on one occasion I was aware of geometric symbols surrounding me. On this occasion I was feeling very relaxed almost to the point of falling asleep when I became conscious of someone very near to me on my right side. My ear and face began to feel warm and tingle. I started to smell cigarette smoke (which

I did not like, as both my parents had smoked when I was a child) and it took me back to my childhood. I then saw a Mars bar—it was just there in my third eye. My thoughts then turned to my uncle who had sexually abused me. He used to buy me chocolate bars every Friday for being a good girl and keeping the secret. I started to question—could this presence be him. The next image that came into my mind was white pumps or trainers as they are now called. It was confirmation, as he used to wear white pumps and an old overcoat. I remember my whole body started to shake uncontrollably as an overpowering sadness engulfed me. I knew he was asking for forgiveness and in my panic, I just wanted him to go away. I was unprepared and had never even considered that he might be sorry for his actions. I started to cry and could not stop as all the hurt and all the pain became so real again. The session had to end. I shared with the therapist that I had experienced a presence relating to my past, thankfully as an experienced therapist she just allowed me to be still and reflect on what had just taken place.

The encounter was so real it remained with me for days. Since that day, I have never experienced anything like it, despite receiving many more sound massage treatments.

I now try to use some method of sound healing daily by listening to the singing bowls on CDs whilst I am writing. This helps to produce both a sense of calmness and clarity.

I also play the gongs both for my own personal pleasure and healing, and for my clients. They share a similar philosophy to sound massage with the singing bowls. The gong promotes creativity and allows us to get in touch with the playful child or inner child, which has often been neglected due to our childhood and the continuous restriction we place on ourselves. It allows us to be open and free to step out of our boundaries and limitations.

Through the gongs resonating within us, the sound of the gong changes as it reflects our inner state of being, which the gong identifies by picking up our emotions such as anger, happiness, love, sensitivity and happiness. Listening to the gongs can change our mood almost instantly from negative to positive. I have witnessed the effect of gongs on others as they enter the gong session as lions and then leave as lambs.

I have used the gong on occasions to release tension from my body, as the gongs rhythmically bring the inner tension or stress encapsulated within me to the point of surrender or no return, letting go as the gong beat increases in speed and volume to reach its climax. Leaving me feeling calmer and free of the negative emotions and stress.

Crystal Healing

As you are aware all life is connected through vibrations, which are transmitted from every plant, animal, human and also from crystals. Matter or energy is not static but an abundance of moving particles of atoms and molecules radiating light, heat and colour. It is this vibration of life that connects us all, as we interact with each other. An awareness of this subtle energy enables us to attract good vibrations whilst protecting ourselves from bad or negative energy. This vital energy is recognised by many healing therapies, which were instrumental in my recovery program. The Chinese call it Chi, the Indian Ayurvedic system refers to it as Prana, Christians speak of the Holy Spirit. When this life energy becomes blocked disharmony is caused between the body, mind and soul and a state of disharmony or disease follows. These blocks of energy are the consequence of a variety things, mainly our modern stressful lifestyles, bad diet, air pollution, additives and chemicals contained in our food, lack of natural light and negative thought patterns.

I have a great respect for crystals and relate to them in many ways. There are crystals in almost every room of my home. Many are positioned to extend their energetic force to those who enter the room or space. With practice you can feel the vibration that crystals emit by holding a crystal in your hand and connecting to its gentle frequency. Crystals act as both a preventative and curative form of therapy, which generate healing vibrations within the body's energy field. These powerful vibrations and frequencies can heal, balance and attune the body, mind and spirit.

Crystals have been a source of healing by traditional medicine people and Shamanism (an ancient healing tradition) around the world for thousands of years. The use of crystals as a healing modality has been recorded as far back as 3,000 years in Chinese texts. Ayurvedic texts from India also record their power and methods used. The Bible has over 200 references to crystals.

Crystals take millions of years to evolve. They are formed in the earth's surface and have their own unique resonance or vibration. They vary in shape, colour and size. Each crystal has an individual precise atomic arrangement.

Over the centuries crystals have been used to attract solar rays, Today's high advanced technology and communication systems are associated with crystals in the form of the silicon chip, along with the quartz crystals in watches to the development of lasers. Scientific research into the properties of crystals is ongoing. Recent research into quartz demonstrates that crystals increase the frequency of light passed through them. This has been an established belief of all crystal healers throughout history who have worked with their own intuition and inner knowing of the healing power of crystals.

The benefits of crystals are as numerous as the crystals themselves. They can improve your general state of health by removing or reducing symptoms of disease. They are an excellent tool for motivating change to lifestyle choices and negative thought processes that we all succumb to, especially regarding our past childhood experiences.

When I started to accept and connect to my Inner Child, crystals played a significant role. As a child I did not have many toys or possessions, crystals provided a route for me to discover the feeling of possessing lots of beautiful, colourful crystals. The crystal became the toys I never had as a child. It is not easy to describe in words the feelings they generated. It was almost like I was a child in a sweet shop when I was in the presence of crystals. I would save for months to purchase a specific crystal I felt drawn to.

My involvement with crystals initially came through my Reiki attunements. My Reiki Master's home was full of beautiful crystals she used them during the Reiki attunements and encouraged her students to work with them. She gave me my first crystal, a rose quartz crystal, which is linked to love.

Even if you do not resonate with the concept of crystal healing, in an attempt to be more open minded I suggest that you purchase a singular crystal and start to work with it. You can choose a crystal for its specific health problem or ailment or simply because you feel drawn to it. There will always be a special crystal that attracts your attention. You can also select a crystal for another person. I choose a crystal, usually a rose quartz crystal and dedicate it to the person I want to send healing to whether it be physical or emotional. In the case of my mother, I have a picture of her when she appeared to be happy, I placed the rose quartz crystal on her photograph and ask that love will surround her and bring her the happiness that she is desperately searching for.

Crystals can play an essential part in your healing journey, as they are effective in emitting positive energy. You can meditate with crystals, you can place them around your home, carry them in your purse or wear them as jewellery.

There are specific crystals that are especially effective when working with past trauma especially relating to childhood and the Inner Child. They are referred to as bridge crystals. They are characterised by having a smaller crystal or crystals protruding from the larger crystal. If the point of the crystal is fairly large and is situated equally within the body of the crystal and outside the crystal it is referred to as a bridge crystal whereas if the smaller crystal is embedded more into the body of the larger crystal, with more inside the large crystal, it is referred to as the Inner Child crystal.

The phrase 'bridge crystal' and 'Inner Child crystal' are used interchangeably. They are helpful in any area you feel might need a bridge to connect to. They are powerful in helping you get in touch with your Inner Child bridging the gap between your adult self (outer self) and your Inner Child (inner self).

Specific crystals for working with the Inner Child.

Blue Chalcedony is also a crystal associated with healing the Inner Child.

Rhodochrosite heals deep emotional trauma relating to childhood

Yellow calcite promotes confidence fun and play

Dioptase is used where there is a need for forgiveness of both self and others

As a Reiki practitioner I started to work more with crystals, I purchased several crystals and would meditate with them and use them during my self-healing sessions. I also used chakra crystals, which I would place on the person during a Reiki session. These are specific crystals that vary in colour. The purpose of laying crystals is to release emotional, mental and spiritual blocks to all aspects relating to health. During a Reiki treatment or a sound massage treatment, which involves using crystals, it is not unusual for the person to experience a great release of emotional baggage resulting in the need to talk and share the past trauma that they have endured.

It is believed that the interaction between the crystals and chakras will return the chakras into a healthy vibration, which can then infuse healing and balance to the part of the body the chakra represents.

Crystal Dedication

This is a general dedication for any crystal so you could ask for whatever you want it to be used for, however as it is going to be used to promote healing of body, mind and spirit, I suggest that you ask it to be used to erase childhood trauma.

Cleanse your crystal under cold running water and leave to dry naturally.

Find a quiet space. Hold the crystal in your left hand. Hover the right hand over the crystal in your left hand, then say

"I ask the crystal to work for the Highest Good of the Crystal. I ask the Angel of the Crystal to oversee the work of the Crystal to the Highest Good."

"I ask the crystal for…"—make your request.

Then say

"I thank the crystal for working for the Highest Good."

"I thank the Angel of the Crystal for overseeing the work of the Crystal to the Highest Good."

"Thank you."

Your crystal is now dedicated.

You can also use your own words to dedicate the crystal. It is the power of intention that is important.

Should you wish to change your dedication you can re-dedicate your crystal by using the crystal dedication and changing your request.

Crystal Cleansing

It is important to cleanse your crystals regularly to ensure that they perform at their highest frequency. Crystals naturally pick up energy from the environment they are placed in. There is no difference between good or bad energy; it is still only energy. This is illustrated in the fact that the Native American Indians used the crystal Obsidian as arrowheads whilst the healers placed Obsidian to ease stomach pain. When we cleanse them, it is not an attempt to discharge negative energy, it is to release energy build up allowing the crystal to be super charged and more effective in its healing role.

There are many cleansing methods to cleanse your crystals

Submerging the crystals in a bowl containing a drop of mild detergent for about thirty minutes. Rinse them thoroughly and either let them dry naturally or gently pat them dry with a soft cloth.

Running water—hold the crystal under running water for a

few minutes.

Sunlight—place your crystals in direct sunlight but be mindful that quartz crystals can be a fire risk, so don't leave quartz crystals unattended. You can also dry your crystals with sunlight after washing them

Moonlight—place your crystals under the light of the moon, especially effective when there is a full moon.

Incense burn frankincense sandalwood and sage smoke, waft over your crystals

Bury your crystals in the earth and leave for at least a week underground. Bury the crystals when it is a full moon and remove during a new moon

Crystal clusters—place your crystals on a bed of amethyst or quartz cluster.

Sound—clears your crystals of negative vibrations by using drumming or chanting. Tibetan bells and bowls played over crystals are also effective for discharging negative vibrations.

Breathing on your crystals is another cleansing technique.

Angel Therapy

The concept of angels is as old as time itself; all major religions refer to Angels. Angel therapy is a non-denominational spiritual healing method that involves working with guardian angels and archangels, to heal and harmonise every aspect of life. Along with your own guardian angel, there are three specific archangels, which work intimately with your Inner Child: Archangel Haniel. Archangel Metatron and Mary Mother of all Angels.

I deliberated long and hard if I should include Angel Therapy, It may be something that you cannot comprehend, which I accept as it opens up an entirely new way of thinking and living and involves change. I believe that only when you are open enough to accept that angels do exist, only then will it be beneficial to engage with the suggested activities.

I believe my first encounter with angels was when I was very young. I used to see my angel shadow on the bedroom door, she was always accompanied with white light. It was only during my involvement with Reiki, that I remembered her nighttime visits and the memory came flooding back.

Whilst I was still living with both my parents I almost drowned. It was a Sunday as both my parents were at home. I had gone out with a friend with the aim of fishing at the local reservoir. We had one green fishing net on a long stick. I stood on what I thought was solid ground and ended up in deep water. I remember thrashing around and screaming as the water engulfed me, as I could not swim.

The next thing I remember was an unexplained force lifting me out of the water and placing me next to my friend. She told me I had jumped out of the water. I knew I could not have jumped out of the water as my feet had not touched the bottom of the reservoir, as it was too deep. Looking back now, I do believe that the incident involved my guardian angel protecting me.

It was in 1983 in California that I became interested in angels and brought them into my life. We were staying with my husband's two spinster aunts. On a visit to San Diego, we visited a shop called Collectables, it was full of   porcelain animals, ranging from frogs, owls, pigs, cows, horses etc. I was invited to select something that I would like to start collecting. Looking around I saw a corner dedicated to angels. I chose a white porcelain angel figure. From that day I started collecting angels, and for birthdays and Christmas I would receive more angels. One club Crewe Alexandray became more than merely objects—they generated beauty and created a sense of calmness and love. My collection of angels extended to books and daily reading cards. Following a Reiki session, I would invite the client to choose an angel card; it was always the right card that was selected, and many clients reported that they had followed the angel message with pleasing results.

I believe we all have guardian angels, which have been present with us since the day we were born and during past lifetimes as some authorities advocate. There are many different realms of angels including the archangels, who are omnipotent beings. It is said your guardian angel carries your divine blueprint, they know what your life purpose is and what you are capable of achieving. They can assist you in every aspect of life, but you must first ask for their help and assistance. They will never enforce anything upon you. Angels observe you making bad decisions and offer higher guidance through your conscience, but you must listen. Angels vibrate at a higher twenty-two than we do.

To work with angels, you need to raise your frequencies, which can be achieved in activities that lift your spirit.

There are many ways you can connect with the angelic forces. I would suggest that you start by asking for them to reveal themselves. You need to be open and responsive to them, they often leave you signs such as white feathers.

Several years ago, after reading one of Diana Cooper's books about angels I decided that I wanted to know the name of my guardian angel. I remember the feeling of anticipation as I prepared for the revelation. I followed the book's instruction and did the meditation. I was disappointed that no name in flashing lights appeared, no neon sign flashed in my mind with the name of my angel or angels as I had read that everyone has two guardian angels. As always, I thought I had done it wrong, and it was my fault that the name of my guardian angel had not been revealed to me. I decided not to do the meditation again that evening, I would try it again the following day. During the night I was awoken by what I can only describe as a voice. it simply said, "I am Stuart", then a female voice said "I am Eloise". I asked if this was correct, Stuart and Eloise, and the answer came back "Yes". To be honest I had not expected an angel to be called Stuart, I had envisaged a name of a more mysterious origin. Regarding the name Eloise, it did strike a chord as my daughter was pregnant and Eloise was one of the names they had chosen if it was a baby girl.

There are many Angel meditations available on YouTube along with books and oracle cards, which will help you to connect to angels if it appeals to you.

Angel Meditation

You will need to set aside a time where you will not be disturbed, ideally choose a place in the house that generates good feelings, a bedroom or the conservatory or a room which overlooks a garden. You may wish to light a candle, play relaxing music, or hold a crystal in your hand and have significant objects around you.

Sit or lie with your back straight.

Ground yourself, which simply means anchoring yourself. Imagine extended roots coming from your feet and travelling down into the depths of the earth. Do not become frustrated if you find it difficult to visualise roots extending, instead repeat the following either verbally or silently "I am safe—I now send roots down into mother earth to ground me with love."

To me Grounding is simply a form of protection from all aspects of energy we are subjected to. As we discussed previously, the Angels function at a much higher frequency and as such we need to remain anchored to the earth's plane. Grounding is used as protection especially with healers and therapists as they interact with people who often have negative energy.

Take some deep breaths, inhale and hold your breath for five seconds then release your breath slowly. Do this several times, placing focus on your breathing. If any thoughts enter your mind thank them for coming, don't give them any power just allow them to pass by as you return your attention to your breathing.

Breathe the colour gold into your being as gold is the colour attributed to angels. Feel this colour travel with your breath into your heart and from there allow it to extend outwards until you are fully cocooned in gold light.

Mentally ask your guardian angel to enter into your aura, the area that extends beyond your personal body. Expect to experience a physical feeling of pressure or a sensation of overwhelming love or a fragrance

Ask your guardian angel to wrap their wings around you and hold you close to them. Relax into their embrace.

If you want to know your guardian angel's name now is the time to ask. Accept whatever name comes into your mind despite how alien it might sound or how ordinary and not what you expected.

Now ask your guardian angel to assist you with whatever problem or challenge you may be facing. Be still and just be.

When you feel, the time is right, thank your guardian angel for coming to connect with you.

Open your eyes and do some stretching movements.

Please do not worry if the meditation does not appear to flow or the visualisation does not work, it is the power of intention and a genuine desire to connect to the angels that is crucial. You may find that in the days that follow you see a name somewhere on a vehicle or poster, in a book or magazine, or one particular name just seems to resonate with you. Trust that instinct; it is your guardian angel trying to communicate with you.

You can use angel cards to receive direct guidance and inspiration and even write to your guardian angels, or the guardian angels of another person. I once wrote a letter to my mother's guardian angels. The purpose behind the activity was to send healing to her. I was aware things were challenging for her, as she was now not speaking to my brother, sister or me. I wanted to do something to help her and to be honest I needed to know I had done everything in my power to heal the past.

Dear Guardian Angels of my mother,

Please will you help my mother to become free of her anger along with the hurt and pain that she is experiencing. Convey to her that she is a precious child who is still searching for love but has not found the source of true love. Please guide her to discover ways to heal her wounds and to be accepting of herself and others.

Send your healing light to melt her frozen heart. May this letter promote the Highest Good of all concerned.

So be it

Thank you

Mirror Work

By now you will be aware that Louise Hay has contributed greatly to my healing journey, I have followed her suggestions relating to my Inner Child and used her Mirror Work therapy, which proved to be one of the most challenging activities I tried, as it was the most revealing in discovering my true self. The concept behind Mirror Work is to enable you to identify the real source of your problems, whether it is related to your health, relationships or finance. The answer to every problem is to learn to love yourself. I can imagine some of the negative thoughts that may emerge from that statement. It sounds too simplistic, right? But how many of us have ever truly loved ourselves due to our insecurities and the need to survive. We uncovered many of the personality traits when we worked with our Inner Child. What Louise Hay's book explained in 250 pages, I will try and convey in a few paragraphs.

If we continue to hide under a mask of illusion and deny the basic need to love ourselves, we will constantly feel that we are not good enough. This negative thought manifests in the way we live our lives. We encounter many problems and life appears to be one long struggle with only the occasional feeling of true contentment, which is temporal as we continually search for this inner acceptance and love, believing that we are not good enough. The only way the cycle of deprivation of the soul can be broken is to stop the negative thoughts patterns we hold about ourselves and start to love our selves unconditionally.

This demands a determined commitment to change the thought patterns we have about ourselves, as whatever we believe is what life presents us with. If we have experienced problems relating to relationships it has links to past experiences and the way, we were socialised especially in our formative years of development within the home environment. If you were bullied at school your belief was that you were not good enough to be part of the in crowd because there was something wrong with you.

Whatever you believe in your subconscious mind about yourself becomes the truth and governs the rules you live by. You need to change the way think about yourself, change your life rules and attitude towards yourself. The first step in this process is learning to love yourself. By believing in your heart that you are worthy of being loved. Whilst this new attitude will not eradicate problems, it is better to view problems as life challenges, which is a positive and nurturing philosophy to adopt. Problems will have less impact and you will attract more positive experiences into your life, therefore avoiding negative consequences.

"Mirror, Mirror on the Wall who is the fairest of us all?"
You Are.

How long do you normally spend in front of a mirror each day as you fix your hair, apply makeup, or if you are a male have a shave? When carrying out your daily routine what do you see? A grey hair? A spot? Smudged mascara? What reflects back to you often results in action and change. How many mirrors are in your home? do you carry a mirror with you to check your appearance throughout the day? Mirrors are useful in looking at our outward appearance. Mirrors can also reflect more than our physical looks and outward appearance; they can reflect our inner thoughts regarding our perception of our self.

The next time you have the opportunity to look into a mirror, look into your eyes and say, "I love and accept you exactly as you are"

Sounds easy enough in theory but in practice it proves for some people impossible. Emotions can arise, such as sadness resulting in tears, anger and frustration. For many people, the first time they look into the mirror in a therapeutic way, cannot look themselves in the eye and tell themselves that they are loved. Initially I found the mirror activity a major challenge. I simply could not say those three words "I love you". It also served as a good barometer of my love and regard for myself. The mirror will be a good tool to monitor your progress. It is a practice that you can include in your daily routine, which is included in the Inner Child Detox Program. It is an excellent tool for building your self-esteem and self-worth. Each time you pass a mirror stop and look into your eyes, aloud or silently say something positive about yourself. You will be surprised how this instigates change. Positive words produce positive feelings and positive feelings are linked to love.

Daily Mirror Mirroring

> *How you start your day is often how you, live your life*—Louise Hay.

The first hour of the day sets the pattern for the entire day. Many people chose to say prayers and meditate early in the morning, which greatly impacts on their day.

A question for you

What are your first thoughts on waking? Are they positive affirmations as you count all your many blessings or are they negative thoughts about all the things that are not working in your life and the problems this created?

By including mirror work into your daily routine, you can expect to have a more productive and enjoyable day along with assisting in your quest of loving yourself and your Inner Child.

Upon waking allow your thoughts to focus on gratitude, think of at least five things that you are grateful for. Tell yourself that it is going to be a good day because you deserve it.

In the bathroom mirror look deeply into your eyes and smile back at the reflection of your beautiful, precious and happy self.

As you look at yourself, say "*Good morning (name) I really do love you. Today is going to be a great day with lots of good things to enjoy.*"

You can use any positive affirmations that appeal to you. Ideally say the affirmations aloud and place your hand on your throat to maximise the impact of the words. and also clear your throat chakra of any blockages.

During the day every time you visit the bathroom and see yourself in the mirror, or pass a window where you see your reflection, repeat the affirmations you had selected in the morning, or if there are others present silently say something positive to yourself and smile at the image reflected back in the mirror. Aim to say the affirmations at least twenty times a day. Before you go to bed at night look in the mirror and stare into the eyes that reflect you. Say a night affirmation such as:

> *"You have made a lot of progress today in changing your thought patterns reflected in your words and actions.*
>
> *I love you and always have, and always will, tomorrow is going to be another great day."*

There are no right or wrong affirmations. You can use your own and the only stipulation is that they are positive, sincere and they come from your heart.

The Healing Code

The definition of The Healing Code is a branch of alternative medicine, which focuses on the use of the human energy field for healing. *The Healing Code*, was discovered by Dr Alex Loyd and the book was co- authored by Ben Johnson in 2001. year a self-administered technique, which involves the use of your fingertips of both hands pointing towards one or more of the four different energy centres of the body that were previously unknown. The science behind it is, when you employ the Healing Code on yourself, the internal stress caused by cellular memories completely disappears, along with disease. There is substantial research that claims that using the Healing Code is effective in reducing cellular stress, which brings the body back into a state of balance. The findings are the result of using the Heart Rate Variability, the only reliable medical apparatus for measuring stress in the nervous system.

The philosophy behind the Healing Codes is summed up in three things:

1 – There is one thing that will heal any problem in your life. It is the immune system

2 – There is one thing that will turn off the immune system. That is stress.

3 – There is one thing that can turn back on the immune system.

The Healing Code - Dr Alex Loyd advocates that everyone is born with a miraculous healing system in his or her body that can heal physical and non-physical issues that a person may have. They argue that there is no disease or illness that a healthy operating immune system cannot heal. They explain that if we have this inner source of healing in the immune system the reason why we ever experience problems is because of stress.

If you accept that the immune system is capable of healing all issues in our lives, then there must be something that prevents the immune system from carrying out its healing properties. Stress must then be the underlying cause of all illness and disease. The link between stress and health has been acknowledged within the medical profession for many years.

With the daily practice of applying the Healing Code you activate your immune system. "When your immune system is working correctly it's impossible to get sick"—Dr Alex Loyd. Even if you are already suffering poor health once you remove the internal stress caused by destructive cellular memories your body will function in the way it was designed to do, and there is no disease or illness that the body is incapable of healing.

There is an abundance of testimonials, which testify to miraculous healings attributed to the healing codes including cancer, AIDS, diabetes, heart disease, arthritis and uterine fibroids. It is also a healing balm for psychological problems including anxiety, depression and other facets of mental illness. The technique is so easy to administer, in the book entitled *The Healing Code* it is said that children as young as seven are using the Healing Code technique daily.

Mark Victor Hansen, the author of the best-selling book *Chicken Soup for the Soul* states "Dr Alex Loyd has the defining healing technology in the world today. It will revolutionise health. It is the easiest way to get well and stay well fast. Dr Alex Loyd may well be the Albert Schweitzer of our time".

I was initially introduced to the Healing Codes by a client, who came to the clinic. She had been using the healing codes to assist with her insecurities and long-term depression. She had sought the assistance of many other therapies in the past, which had little effect. She claimed that her depression was improving and that her eating habits were changing and the need for carbohydrates, mainly chocolate, had diminished. The next time she came to the clinic she brought her copy of the book. I was impressed with the philosophy contained in the book as it reinforced my belief in energy medicine.

I bought a copy of the book and started doing the *Six Minute Ritual*, which includes positioning your hands and fingers around your face and jaw, whilst reciting the sacred prayer. Not only did I experience a tingling sensation in my fingers and face, within a short time I started to feel a shift in my attitude to things, I became more aware of my own personal needs as I worked with my Inner Child. I continue to practice the healing codes on a regular basis as a precautionary tool for maintaining my physical and emotional health.

I also attended a workshop relating to the Healing Codes. It was there that I heard about other ways the healing codes can be engaged to bring about change and balance. A man explained that his problem or need was to sell his house, apparently it had been on the market for over a year, he was about to lose the deposit that he had put on a new property. When he started to implement the healing code, he declared within a week that the house had been sold; he was convinced that it was the result of practicing Healing Code. Another client had been using the healing code to work on her uterine fibroids successfully. I am also aware of people who claim they have used the Healing Code to heal breast cancer, diabetes, eating disorders and prostate cancer.

The healing techniques requires only six minutes of your time, the more times you are able to perform it during the day the quicker you can expect to see the results.

Diagrams of the hand positions can be found online or in the book *The Healing Code.*

The hand positions are the same for whatever issue you want to work on. The prayer can be adapted to highlight your health problem or issue. This is the prayer I used in relation to my inner child.

I ask that all known and unknown negative images, unhealthy beliefs and all physical issues related to my childhood, would be found, opened and healed by filling me with the light and love of God. I also pray that the effectiveness of this healing will be increased by 100 times or more.

Whilst researching the healing codes for the purpose of this book I came across more than one critical appraisal of the therapy. My response and recommendation to you is to adopt an open mind and carry out the self-healing practice for a week. If the therapy works you will be convinced of its healing properties like me. If it doesn't what have you to lose? Six minutes of your day.

Energy Medicine by Donna Eden

"Your body is designed to heal itself. The ability of a body to maintain its health and overcome illness is, in fact, amongst nature's most remarkable feats, taken *from Energy Medicine,* Donna Eden and David Feinstein's, award winning guide to Energy Medicine.

If there is one person who encapsulates the whole essence of energy healing, it is Donna Eden. I count myself very blessed to have been able to attend a workshop she held, when she visited Manchester from the States. She explained the realms of energy medicine in such a realistic and practical way, we were able to observe the forces of energy and learn how to balance our own energy field and release blocked energy. Since that day I have been using her techniques daily, they are part of my daily routine, I see them as important as eating breakfast or taking a shower in fact in the shower is where I carry out one of her energy shifting techniques.

Donna Eden is one of the most inspirational people I have ever met. By carrying out her recommendations and working with my energy fields I learnt how to move blocked energy pathways within my physical body. I also became aware of the importance of removing emotional blockages, which were so important in my recovery.

She firmly believes that we are capable of healing our own bodies, she states "Put healing into good hands—Your Own". Due to my reticence to involve anyone in relation to my emotional health, I was convinced that this was going to hold a key to unlocking my emotional baggage. How did I know that as I sat waiting for her to appear on stage that this was going to be life changing? It was something deep inside—an inner knowing. Her personality and demeanour were electrifying as she demonstrated a host of energy balancing techniques, which we were able to perform on ourselves.

During the evening I purchased two of her books, which contained illustrated diagrams of how to connect and move the energy fields.

I also used Donna Eden's DVDs *Energy Medicine, The Essential Technique* as a source of instruction.

When she was in her late thirties, she began to direct her own energies to heal herself of multiple sclerosis.

She claims that energy medicine and its benefits are not reserved for medically trained doctors, alternative health experts and gifted healers. She advocates that we all have the ability to tap into our life force energy to create a fundamental mind-body shift that can transform our lives.

In energy medicine, energy is the medicine and energy, is also the patient. With energy as the medicine, the natural vital life force that is your birth right can be harnessed and directed to cure your ills and uplift your spirit. With energy as the patient, you can restore energies that have become weak, disturbed and out of balance and heal your body as a consequence.

Energy Medicine is available to anyone. It involves

straightforward, easy to learn techniques, which you can apply daily, as flow, balance and harmony can be non-invasively restored and maintained within your body system by:

Tapping, massaging or holding specific energy points on the skin

Tapping or swirling your hand above your skin along specific energy pathways

Practicing exercises or postures designed to bring a feeling of calm and renewal

Surrounding an area with healing energies

There are specific procedures that you can enlist for both physical and emotional issues, which are described in detail in her books. Her techniques can be learnt and used when needed. You can use the book as a reference to identify the energy moving remedy for a specific problem you are encountering, a deep emotional issue, or a traumatic incident that you have experienced.

Due to copyright restrictions, it is not possible to print diagrams of the techniques from her books and material that I have used.

In an attempt to introduce you to Donna Eden's energy work I have selected three simple techniques that can be described in text.

Fear Tap

It can be used anytime you're feeling anxious or frightened, it can also help to change underlying problems of long-standing phobias. It requires tapping an energy point located on the back of your hand. Tapping on these energy points can shift energies of fear and gently alleviate unwanted thoughts and the emotions associated with it.

When you are afraid it creates stress, agitation and exhaustion. It can be related to a specific fear, or it can be a generalised irrational fear such as attending an interview or exams.

- Locate the area on the back of your hand halfway between your wrist and fingers, between your little finger and ring finger.
- Tap this area with two or three fingers for about 30 seconds to a minute. At the same time breathe in through your nose and out through your mouth. Switch hands and repeat.
- Another method is to place your hand over your heart and tap on it.

The Four Thumps

The four specific points used in this technique are to recharge your batteries, they help boost your immune system, balance electrolytes, help with metabolism of food, reduce toxins and stress and provide clarity of thoughts.

- Using both hands place the pads of your fingers beneath your cheekbone next to your nose. Thump firmly for 15 seconds. This helps to drain sinuses and clear the lymph glands in the neck. It can also release tension and reduce excessive worry.
- Place your fingers on your collarbone and move them inwards towards the U-shaped notch on the top of your breastbone. Move your fingers to the bottom of the U. Then move your fingers to the left and the right and thump firmly for 10 to 15 seconds.
- Place your fingers of either hand in the centre of your sternum (chest) on your thymus gland. Thump firmly for about 10 to 15 seconds.
- Locate the neurolymphatic spleen point beneath the breasts and one rib down, place one hand under each breast and thump firmly with your fingers or knuckles 10 to 15 seconds.

This activity is good to do in the morning when you are taking a shower.

Along with the exercises above I used other techniques, which connect to the discharging of painful memories linked to my childhood. She describes the painful destructive memories as land mines that are left in the ground after a war, the defensive responses you adopt during the trauma need to be defused and cleared for life to be fully restored. Through the following exercise you can mobilise energy that will open you up to letting go of the stored negative energy that is responsible for your habits, which are programmed into your mind.

This learnt coping strategy also dictates how you respond to further life events, through learnt behaviour patterns you have learnt in the quest to survive the trauma, which in turn is restricting you from attaining your true potential.

Defusing Traumatic Residue

- Select a memory from the past that is painful to you or has an emotional grip on you.
- Place your fingers of both hands on your forehead and your thumbs on the temples next to your eyes. Stretch the skin using your fingers and keep the thumbs still. Bring your fingers back to the neurovascular point on your forehead and rest. To find the neurovascular point, find the two bumps on your forehead directly over your eyes. Do this for at least two minutes. Breathe deeply in through your nose and out through your mouth.

You can also visualise the memory but if this proves too difficult, simply say an affirmation "I consciously release this negative destructive memory, let it go, let it flow". There are many other activities illustrated in her books that you can carry out on a daily basis.

HO'OPONOPONO

I was introduced to Ho'oponopno through a client who had read the book called *Zero Limits* by Joe Vitale and Dr Ihaleakala Hew Len. The latter was a Hawaiian therapist who had cured an entire ward of mentally ill criminals without speaking to any of them. By simply reviewing the patient's file he healed them by healing himself first. When Joe Vitale heard of this extraordinary healing method, he began a mission to find out more about the virtues of Ho'oponopno and to meet this amazing Hawaiian doctor. The book along with workshops conducted by Dr Hew Len and Joe Vitale became available in the USA and the practice of Ho'oponopno flourished throughout the States. It is a self-taught therapy that requires no intervention from a practitioner, making it attractive to me as a source of realising the toxic memories of my childhood.

I bought the book and discovered that the name Ho'oponopono means 'to make or rectify an error' according to the ancient Hawaiians.

Error rises from thoughts that are tainted by painful memories of the past. Ho'oponopono offers a different a way to release the energy of these painful thoughts, errors and memories, which cause imbalance and disease. It is a process of letting go of toxic energies within you and to allow the impact of divine thoughts, words deeds and actions to promote wellbeing

Ho'oponopono taught me a great lesson in forgiveness, once it became part of my daily routine. I use it to help clear away the hurts and pain that I was experiencing. The word PONO doesn't translate well into English, words like congruency, calmness and harmony and the concept that everything is right in the world or being totally at peace with a person or situation that there is no need for words to be exchanged. Ho'oponopono means to become doubly PONO.

The ancient Hawaiians believed and taught it was important

to feel calm and clear and promote ways of being in harmony with everyone around them at all times. So they practiced Ho'oponopono daily, allowing them to stay clear of any resentment, anger or hurt that caused a blocked energy within their body. The practice of Ho'oponopono includes gaining wisdom from the negative experience. You are free to make the choice to re-establish a friendship with the person who hurt you or decline—the choice is yours.

The philosophy behind Ho 'oponopono struck a chord with me as I was working with my Inner Child along with initiating methods of letting go of the pain and shame associated with my childhood. It was also at a Ho'oponopono workshop that I learnt about narcissistic personality disorder traits, which I was able to identify in my mother. I believe the concept of Ho'oponopono came to me at the right time on my healing journey, I was able to see my mother as a victim of a personality disorder, which allowed me to forgive her and learn to start loving myself.

The Philosophy of Ho'oponopono

In an attempt to try and understand how by healing yourself you can heal others the reason as in the case of Dr Hew Len is that there is no "out there" everything that you hear, see, every person you meet, you experience in your mind, you only think it is "out there" detaching you from any responsibility. The whole philosophy of Ho'oponopono is the reverse; you are responsible for everything you think and everything that comes to your attention.

When watching the news or reading about the dilemma of others you are confronted with negativity, you are responsible for their plight and hardship. This is a difficult truth to accept but if you accept your responsibility, it means that you can actively clear it, clean it, and through forgiveness change it.

There are four important elements to the healing: Repentance,

Forgiveness, Gratitude and Love.

I am Sorry

To accept that you are responsible for everything that enters your mind is not the easiest thing to do and the realisation can be painful and initially you are likely to resist. It is not logical thinking that you are responsible for anything out of your control.

In an attempt to accept your responsibility, choose a problem or an issue that you have, concerning relationships, addictions, or personality issues, such as anger health problems, anything that involves you. Then bring the issue to mind and say, "I am sorry". You can expand the word sorry "I feel truly responsible for the [issue] I am truly sorry that something in my mind has caused this".

Forgiveness

Repeat the words "please forgive me" and mean it. It is irrelevant who you are asking to forgive you, just keep on repeating the words "Please forgive me".

Gratitude

Say "Thank You", learn to live in a state in constant gratitude. It does not need to be addressed to one specific source, you can thank God, the universe, angels, yourself for being the best you can be, just keep saying thank you.

I Love You

Love is the most powerful force in life, try and live in a cocoon of love, surround yourself with loving feelings. Say "I love you" to everything; material things, your body, your mind, your spirit, the air you breathe, the water you drink, the food you eat, and really mean it.

It is beyond the remit of my book to be able to give you an in-depth account of the therapy, if you feel that Ho'oponopono could help you on your healing journey I urge you to read the book entitled *Zero Limits—The Secret Hawaiian System for Wealth Health and Peace* by Joe Vitale.

Apart from using my daily mantras in connection to my own personal healing with my Inner Child, I also use the mantras to clear and cleanse in my work situation as I cleared prior to a colonic treatment or sound massage believing that the treatments are more effective having dispersed negative energy.

For several months I listened to a CD based on the ancient traditional healing of the Hawaiians. I played the CD each night as I went to sleep. This was possible by using Pillow Talk, the speaker connected to my phone. It also gives me the opportunity to listen to other inspirational music and meditations. Admittedly I often fall asleep but in the case of the Inner Child meditation it works on the subliminal, the subconscious mind so it is still effective if you do fall asleep.

Flower Essences

My first encounter with flower essences came through a lady I met on a training course relating to an energy machine I had purchased. She was a trained Bach flower essence therapist and homeopath who made me a remedy to help with my food intolerances.

Flower essences as a healing act was introduced in modern times by Dr Edward Bach. He was born in 1886 near Birmingham. He was trained as a physician and spent many years as bacteriologist focusing on chronic disease. He became disenchanted with orthodox medicine and the notion of alleviating symptoms of disease rather than the cause of disease. He started to explore vaccine therapy along with homeopathy and the principle of treating the whole person. Through his findings, Bach came to believe that emotional states were the cause of physical disease.

He began to catalogue different personality types which led to certain patterns of health imbalances. In 1930 Bach gave up his medical practice and spent the final six years of his life in the fields around his home exploring various flowers and their effect on human emotions and health. He is reported to have been a sensitive, intuitive soul who was drawn to certain plants and determined their therapeutic value by using them on himself. He ultimately promoted thirty- eight healing flowers, that make up the Bach Flower Remedies.

Bach offered no scientific explanation as to how flower essences work. He did however leave hundreds of case studies detailing the positive effects of flower remedies. For many years his healing art and formulas remained obscured until the 1970s and 1980s when other individuals around the globe started to research and develop flower essences. From small beginnings there is now a host of reputable companies that make and sell flower essences.

Even today there are still no scientific explanation as to why and how flower essences work. Pharmaceutical medicines, herbs and nutritional supplements can all be explained due to causing chemical reactions in the body, which can be detected and monitored. Flower essences like, homeopathy and acupuncture, are energetic medicines. Theoretically what energy medicine does is act like a trigger for the body's own ability to heal. In relation to flower essence the common belief is that the energetic pattern of the flower essence is similar to the energetic pattern of the individual's emotional state. The body responds to the stimulus of the flower essences and works by bringing the body back into balance.

Throughout the years I have had clients and friends who used flower essences on a regular basis. Whilst you do not need to be qualified to use the flower essence, there are trained therapists who during a consultation will intuitively select the most beneficial essences for you. The flower essences are also sold in both health shops and on- line. There are also questionnaires you can complete, which will direct you to the essences that will be the most beneficial to you. The amazing thing about flower essences is that it works primarily on your emotional health, which makes it an essential ingredient to healing the emotional trauma that has been inflicted on the Inner Child.

I was so fascinated with flower essences that I embarked on a study course written by Stefan Ball, which is recommended by The Bach Centre. It is an excellent workbook with case studies for you to assess and then recommend which flower essence would be the most helpful at that given time. The correct answers are all contained in the book, which include descriptions of all the thirty- eight Bach flower essences.

I have taken the following analogy in an attempt to convey to you how flower essences work. It is taken from the book. *The Flower Remedy* by Jeffrey Garson Shapiro.

As I personally use tuning forks on family and friends the explanation resonated with me.

The room represents the body, and the first tuning fork is the flower essences, and the second matching tuning fork represents the emotional states.

One enters the room holding a tuning fork. In this room the walls are lined with many tuning forks, each one is a different musical note. If you strike the fork being held it will start to vibrate. Nothing will happen to any of the other forks in the room except if there is one fork of the same note, it too will start to vibrate.

This causes the emotional body to become balanced and receptive.

I have also used flower essences that have been prepared by qualified practitioners who during a consultation have identified my personality type along with my thought patterns, which indicated areas pertaining to my emotional health that were out of balance. Flower essences are safe and have no side effects, they can even be used on children. Healing the Inner Child has been the focus of my recovery and I truly believe that using the flower essences over the years has helped me to connect with my Inner Child due to the gentle nurturing effect that they create. Star of Bethlehem is used for childhood trauma; Centaury restores the qualities of inner strength and self-determination; Crab apple works as a cleansing remedy both inside and outside

I do hope by now you are becoming aware of the importance of healing your Inner Child. It is one of the most empowering things you can do on your journey of recovery. It allows us work with a higher consciousness and an acceptance of our childhood, which comes about by the clearing of deep emotional hurts and imbalances.

By releasing fear and lack of self-love along with other ego patterns we can start to heal our Inner Child. This will allow us to experience more joy, harmony, peace and love into our lives. Bringing deep emotional healing and transformation of the past will create a new future by resolving our unhealed issues. This will allow us to move forward and change our life for the better. By feeling more joy and happiness our healed Inner Child will create a more loving experience through our positive thoughts and emotions.

Emotional Freedom Tapping

A major tool I want to promote to you is emotional freedom tapping. As the name indicates it erases painful emotions that are attached to traumatic or hurtful experiences that we have encountered especially in relation to childhood memories that are locked deep within our cellular memories. It is also a self-administered therapy, which can be learnt and validated by your individual progress in erasing the pain and hurt associated with an incident. The memory will never be lost but is replaced by an inner acceptance and love for yourself by taking away the negativity associated with the event and allowing you to move away from the self-limiting beliefs you carry about yourself. These keep you from discovering your true self and working to promote your full potential by not believing in or loving yourself. By now you will understand how the majority of therapies we have discussed all focus on moving energy along the meridians or energy pathways.

Emotional Freedom Tapping or EFT as it often referred to, is a combination of both ancient Chinese acupuncture and modern psychology that works to physically alter your brain energy system and body in one easy to learn tapping sequence, which consists of tapping with your fingertips on specific meridians while talking through traumatic memories and a wide range of emotions.

According to Dr Dawson Church "Acupoints tapping sends signals directly to the stress centres of the mid-brain, not mediated by the frontal lobes [the thinking part, active in talk therapy]" Due to EFT being able to access both the body and mind he likens it to receiving a massage during a psychotherapy session.

The original founder of the tapping technique was the late Dr Roger Callahan, who discovered that by tapping on a meridian point people started to feel better. This was initially discovered by helping a lady called Mary to conquer her fear of water.

She had received eighteen months of conventional therapy to eradicate her fear with no effect. She described her phobia as "an awful feeling in her stomach." It is said that Dr Callahan had a brain wave to ask Mary to think of the fear of water whilst tapping under her eye, which according to ancient body mapping of the meridians is directly linked to the stomach. With no further intervention Mary was completely cured of her water phobia. Following Mary's success Dr Callahan began experimenting with tapping various meridian points. His findings were initially known as "Callahan Techniques" but later became "Thought Field Therapy". The therapy gained momentum and was made available to students wanting to learn more about the tapping technique. One student was Gary Craig a graduate engineer working in insurance sales. With a strong commitment to research and self-improvement, he trained in 1991 in Thought Field Therapy, which he evolved into Emotional Freedom Tapping as is recognised today. It is estimated that over 10 million people worldwide have used tapping. It is amazing how quickly it can alleviate issues like depression, anxiety and insomnia, physical pain even preventing illness.

I have first-hand experience how effective the procedure is. My eldest daughter developed a phobia about flying due to a bad experience she encountered whilst taking an internal flight in America when the plane had to make an emergency landing. Thankfully the plane landed safely. However, this had a profound effect on her resulting in her declaring that she would never fly again.

It was her young son who eventually put pressure on her to fly, as he wanted to go to Florida. As a Christmas gift she received a fear of flying course. One of the techniques she learnt on the course was EFT. I do not think she will ever enjoy flying but now it no longer prevents her from travelling. She always uses tapping prior to flying and during the flight.

The basic technique requires you to focus on the negative

emotion that causes you pain when you think about it, it could be a fear, an unresolved problem a physical condition in fact there is nothing that cannot benefit by applying EFT. There are several websites along with demonstrations on YouTube that show how to apply EFT in relation to a specific problem or issue.

They include issues with:
- Anger
- Depression
- Digestive problems
- Anxiety
- Stress
- Panic attacks
- Headaches
- Insomnia

The list is endless.

EFT was a major feature in my recovery especially when I was addressing deep cellular memories that I had suppressed for so long. I urge you to delve more into these amazing techniques. Please do not be put off by its simplicity and lack of scientific data. Complimentary medicines have not the financial resources to instigate major analytical research, which provides quantitative data. There are many research papers that prove the effectiveness of therapies such as EFT, but the source is on a qualitative approach using case studies and individual's opinions rather than statistical evidence. Please do your own research on the Internet, to give you the latest findings.

The question to ask anyone who wants to work with EFT is "What is the issue that is causing you the most pain and hurt?" For me it was the shame and guilt of being identified as a 'dirty bitch' by my mother in relation to the child sexual abuse I had encountered.

Prior to commencing an EFT session, you are asked to rate your issue from one to ten, one being mild, ten being strong.

The basic technique requires you to tap on nine body meridians, whilst placing your mental focus on the problem, fear, hurtful memory, anything that is causing you concern. Tapping on these meridian points while you are concentrating on accepting and resolving the negative emotion will restore your body into a balanced state.

There are many excellent videos demonstrating the technique on YouTube, they all follow a similar sequence pattern, but some include additional meridian points such as the top of the head. I suspect this is due to individual practitioners experimenting by using other meridians and gaining positive results. I have included here the sequence of tapping and the script I devised when I worked with my Inner Child, the script can be adapted, or you can write your own script specifying your own problem or issue.

The occasion I am going to focus on was when my mother called me a dirty bitch. She had said it many times before, but on this occasion, it completely shook me to the depths, her words penetrated so deep that I felt I could not breathe. I felt nauseated and found it hard to stay upright. I was home alone. As I explained earlier, I had rung her as the previous day she had been upset stating that life was not worth living and she wished she could die as no one cared about her. Her mood was no better when I rang her that day. She accused me, and my family of being "shite". I tried to remind her that she had chosen to move away and live in Chester. Her cruel tongue escalated as she told me I was nothing but a dirty bitch and that I used to blackmail my uncle. She reminded me of the sweets and comics he used to buy me. I remember screaming back telling her that I was NOT a dirty bitch. At some point during that conversation, she slammed the phone down.

The ordeal was so traumatic that I can remember every detail associated with it. It was a Tuesday and I had been out on student placement visits and had nipped home for lunch.

During my nurse training we were told that if you ever have to give bad news to relatives regarding a loved one, they will remember every detail about you as if time stood still. That is exactly what my mother's words did to me that day, so many years ago, even today I can, still recall the feelings that it generated.

There are many EFT scripts available on the Internet, which show the location of the nine meridians points to tap. The basic structure always remains the same, but the words can differ each time I carry out an EFT treatment. When I work with a qualified EFT practitioner I recite the given words, however when working on my own I have no set script, the words just flow as they come from my heart and not so much from my head. There is no right or wrong script, there is no perfect script, it is a dialogue with your heart or from your Inner Child that produces results. Remember, as with any therapy, it is the power of intention that is important not the act of getting it right.

What you can expect to gain from a session of EFT again varies from individual to individual, but one thing is guaranteed, there will be a shift within, you may feel immense sadness resulting in tears or uplifted as you feel a sense of love for yourself. I really do not want to predict anything—just go with the flow and trust that the healing will take place where it is needed the most, working on the core or the key issues that are causing you pain.

Emotional Freedom Tapping for Emotional Healing

I have included a script below which I used to connect with my Inner Child.

Karate chop

"Even though I believed I was a dirty bitch as a child I accept and love myself."

Top of head using both hands

"I did not realise that my belief was hurting you my Inner Child."

Eyebrow

"I am sorry that I abandoned you and let you live with the shame."

Under eye

"I am sorry that I deprived you of love and attention just like my mother did to me."

Under nose

"I am sorry that I ignored you when you wanted to be creative and play."

Chin

"I beat you up with negative thoughts and never praised you for anything."

Collarbone

"I was always fearful and afraid of getting into trouble."

Under arm

"I ignored you and abandoned you because I did not know you existed."

Top of head

"I will never hurt you again by ignoring you."

The act of following a session of EFT with positive affirmations is not something that all EFT practitioners or EFT courses promote. However, one EFT practitioner encouraged me to end each of my EFT sessions with a positive tapping sequence. As the purpose of introducing the therapies that have been crucial to my healing, I feel the need to explain the therapies exactly as I experienced them.

Following an EFT sequence as described above I suggest that you affirm some positive affirmations, using the same meridian points start with the Karate chop and work through the sequence. Use affirmations that you would say to a young child or someone you love deeply.

- "I am so proud of the progress you have made today"
- "You are a very special person who deserves only the best"
- "Never forget that you are safe and protected"
- "You are never alone you are supported in every way"
- "You are amazing just the way you are"
- "There is nothing that you cannot achieve"
- "You are precious and loved very much"

You can of course write your own affirmations or use any that have been promoted throughout the book. Whilst they may be difficult at first to repeat with any conviction, they will resonate deep within your cells, and the effect will carry momentum as you discover your true self and recognise what you are really capable of achieving.

The Law of Attraction

The Law of Attraction is not classified as a therapy as such. It is more a way of life governed by a set of laws, which brings rewards when you promote positive thoughts. However, it will also attract negative experiences if you send out negative thoughts—like attracts like. It is based on the belief that people and their thoughts are made of pure energy and the belief that positive energy attracts positive energy whilst negative energy attracts negative energy.

The philosophy grew out of the teachings of Phineas Quimby in the early 19th century. Whilst his work was only in relation to health issues, he never used the term 'Law of Attraction'. His core belief was similar in that he stated, "The trouble is in the mind, for the body is only the house for the mind to dwell in, and we put value on it according to its worth. Therefore, if your mind has been deceived, by some invisible enemy into a belief you have put it into the form of a disease, with or without your knowledge. By my theory or truth, I come into contact with your enemy, and restore you to your health and happiness. This I do partially by talking till I correct the wrong impression and establish the truth, and the truth is the cure".

The Law of Attraction was first printed in a book written by the Russian occultist Helena Blavatsky. By the end of the 19th century, it was being used in every aspect of life, by new thought activists. The twentieth century brought a surge of interest in the subject, resulting in many books being written amongst them in 1984 was Heal Your Life by Louise Hay, which we explored in Part Three - Working with Your Inner Child, along with her affirmations throughout the book.

The Law of Attraction gained a lot of momentum, and in 2006 it received renewed exposure with the release of the film, The Secret, which was made into a book the following year. The author Rhonda Byrne discovered the secret, is the Law of Attraction. She believes that whatever you focus your attention on becomes reality in your life. It is based on the energy that the universe is made of, and the vibrations of that energy.

Returning to the concept of energy, which is the central theme of all the therapies we have discussed previously, its basic rule is that all energy vibrates at different frequencies. Everything is energy including us. Rhonda Byrne promotes the theory that the frequency a person vibrates, is determined by their thoughts and emotions, which attract other things that vibrate at a similar frequency.

With this in mind if you desire something in your life that vibrates at a different frequency, you have to change your own frequency by changing your thoughts. By seeing thoughts as magnets, they will attract all like things that are on the same frequency. To make the Law of Attraction work for you, focus your thoughts on the positive, see a half full glass not a half empty glass. The key to success is to increase the amount of time that you actually feel good, savour that feeling, do more things that bring you pleasure and be grateful until it becomes a way of life.

I have used the Law of Attraction for many years, or I should say I have lived with the Law of Attraction for many years. I am living proof of the effectiveness of the law working in my life. From manifesting dreams and desires to obtaining material objects as big as selling my previous home. I have also seen the Law of Attraction working in the lives of family, friends and clients. There is nothing you cannot achieve with the correct mind set with positive thoughts.

There is lots of further information on the Internet, which will develop your understanding of the Law of Attraction if you feel it is something that would work for you. Rhonda Byrne says, "If you do only one thing with your acquired knowledge of the Secret, use gratitude until it becomes a way of life."

I have read and studied all her books, which are listed in the bibliography. I also found it very inspiring to listen to one of her books called The Power. I bought the CD and then downloaded it on to my phone. I sometimes listen to it whilst doing the ironing or cleaning. I also found it beneficial to listen to her when I was in bed through the Pillow Talk device that I use to listen to my meditative music and meditations.

A quote from Rhonda Byrne:

> *The truth is that the universe has been answering you all your life, but you cannot receive the answers unless you are awake.*

> *Life is supposed to be fun! When you are having fun, you feel great and receive great things! Having fun brings the life you want, and taking things too seriously brings a life you have to take seriously.*

> *Your power is in your thoughts, so stay awake. In other words, remember to remember.*

The Journey by Brandon Bays

The Journey is a globally recognised healing therapy, which promotes physical and emotional healing. This healing modality is attributed to Brandon Bays the founder who was healed completely from a basketball sized tumour in six and half weeks without the use of drugs or surgery. She embarked on a healing journey beyond the scope of known alternative medicine, which she had been involved with for over twenty years.

She believed her life changing experience had to be shared with others and she achieved this by writing, The Journey, which became an international best-selling book. This led to the development of seminars and workshops, which are available through qualified Journey practitioners in 47 different countries. The Journey experience claims that by seeking the truth through the light of your own soul, you can forgive yourself and others and heal once and for all in every aspect of your life.

It is a simple revolutionary set of techniques that free life-long emotional and physical blocks relating to addictions, depression and low self-esteem to chronic pain and illnesses.

It guides us directly to the root cause of long-term problems associated with both the body and mind. It involves an imaginative process that allows us to access and release memories that are held in specific parts of the body. The technique can be used by anyone; there is also a children's edition of her book available.

The Journey is a process that allows you to clear old issues that have held you back in life for years. Using your own infinite wisdom, you can clear old negative memories stored in your cells, which are acting as a barrier to developing your true potential.

The fundamental core of the journey is the need to forgive people who have wronged you in the past and hurt you. Her teachings focus on the realisation that forgiveness is a gift and the key element to healing. The act of forgiveness does not mean that we condone the abusive behaviour. Or allow them to repeat the offensive act. The hurtful deed is probably an unforgivable experience. The Journey process allows you to access buried cellular memories linked to past hurts, and find forgiveness towards yourself, which is a real crucial act if we are ever to attain true healing. Along with forgiving the soul of the person who has deeply wounded you. This frees you from the bondage of suffering.

The concept behind The Journey resonated with me. One of the points The Journey highlights is that every time we repeat our story and recall the event verbally or in our thoughts, we stir up emotions that flood negative energy into every cell of our body. I have proved this to be the case to avoid the pain associated with the sexual abuse and my mother's indifference. I would block it out and not allow myself to attach any emotional value to it. The emotions were suppressed and delivered to every cell of my body and the consequence was I was living a robotic existence devoid of any emotional release. Brandon Bays describes e-motions as really energies in motion.

Her teachings highlight the point that when these emotions are not allowed to be released, they have a major impact on both our physical and mental health. Positive emotions have healing qualities such as feeling loved and valued, whilst negative emotions when constantly being repeated damage the natural healing cycle. Forgiveness disrupts this damaging cycle and allows us to initiate healthier beliefs that are in tune with our highest and deepest healing. We can learn from the actions of animals in the wild, an antelope that has escaped being caught by a predator will automatically shake off the excessive adrenalin that has been generated by the chase.

Whereas humans do not release this excessive energy; we are socialised into keeping it under control and the excessive energy is stored as cellular memories, which in turn affects every decision we make in life as it is influenced by suppressed fear. This prevents us from making choices that are in our best interest. These learnt patterns and behaviour traits prevent us from living creative productive lives.

The Journey gives opportunity to connect to these stored negative emotions from the past and release the stored blocked energy in a positive way. It is a simple and effective way to access innate programs we adopt that consequently rule our lives. It can eradicate old habits and behaviour patterns, which in turn produce more positive actions that allow us to let go of the emotional ties of the past and move forward.

The Program claims to:
- Access old cellular memories
- Feel each and every emotion fully
- Empty out the stored pain
- Clear out the cellular blockages
- Forgive self, others and life
- Never condone abusive behaviours
- Extricate our emotions from our beliefs, and our beliefs and emotions from our behaviours.

There are books and CDs that explain the process, which involves taking an imaginary journey where you meet with those from the past who have hurt you and caused you pain. It enables you to separate your emotions from your behaviour. I have read the book several times and found it helpful. I purchased the CD and have on more than one occasion undertaken the journey, which involves entering a meditative state and visualising going through layers of emotions eventually reaching a campfire where the people who have hurt you are present. You confront them with the pain that they have inflicted on you. In response they too are allowed to contribute and explain why they acted the way they did. It is all resolved with there being no blame attributed to anyone. Forgiveness and a general respect for each other is fostered, resulting in the past or issue having no emotional ties or connection to the one who is taking the journey.

Whilst you can carry out the journey with a trusted friend who can read the text for you and support you during your journey this is not always an option for some people. Thankfully there are qualified Journey practitioners who will work with you, or you can attend a workshop where you can undertake your personal journey with the assistance of qualified practitioners.

Whilst the following techniques are not classed as therapies, I have used them and found them to be a source of help.

Detaching from Negative Feelings

To discharge negative thoughts, which would suddenly transcend, I placed a tight elastic band on my wrist, throughout the day every time a negative thought entered my mind, I pulled at the elastic band a distance from my wrist and then let it go, resulting in slight discomfort. It is amazing how this simple act produced positive results, not only did I become aware of how many times I focused on negative thoughts, I was also able to turn them into positive thoughts. If I hear someone being negative regarding someone else, I listen, but then try and offer a positive thought regarding that person. It often results in the person changing the focus of the conversation away from being negative about another person.

Tapping the Thymus Gland

This was a technique I learnt from an EFT practitioner. When I began to verbally express my suppressed emotional pain, I found it helpful to simply tap my thymus gland, which is located to the left of the sternum in the centre of your chest.

Almost immediately my voice would become calmer and quieter resulting in my breathing returning to a normal rhythm. I could feel the anxiety of the event I was describing decrease in intensity.

Tapping to Register Positive Thoughts

Tapping on the Karate chop on the side of the hand can enforce and extend positive feelings by tapping the positive feeling you are experiencing in that moment into your energy pathway circuit. It then becomes a positive cellular memory. When you recall the scene, it could be the feeling of euphoria that a scene in nature provides or an encounter with a loved one, or words of praise or affection from someone, it does not matter what the act was that generated the positive feeling. It is the feeling in itself that is important and is stored in your cellular memory, which you can access.

Meditation

It is said that everyone has the ability to meditate; it is not a mystical gift that is restricted to spiritual gurus and those in search of spiritual truths. A method of practicing meditation is to use visualisation as a tool. We all use visualisation daily without giving it a second thought.

If I asked you to describe your front door to me, to be able to do this you would automatically visualise the door—the colour, the position of the letter box, the door handle in your third eye, the door becomes real through images in your mind. I use both guided meditations regularly and meditative music to help me to be still and open to clearing away mind chatter that can dominate my thinking.

Therapeutic Breathing or Mindful Breathing

I am no authority on breath work, I know it works for me, from deep breathing exercises to conscious breathing activities in preparation for meditations or working with the Tibetan singing bowls and gongs. The practice of mindful breathing prepares the body and mind to be still. There are many breathing techniques you can try, I have included a breathing activity in the Inner Child Detox.

Morning Meditation

An integral part of my healing journey involves a daily quiet time at the commencement of each day. I have a special place where I go, it is filled with precious artefacts crystals, shells, singing bowls, gongs, pictures and photographs, which generate a peaceful and nurturing environment to spend time in thought and prayer, as I connect to a Higher Being, and awakening of my soul within. "I feel engulfed in the unconditional love my daily connection provides".

This act of reverence is not associated with any secular religion. It is a place where everyone can enter regardless of any religious beliefs.

It is the strength I gather every morning that has enabled me to keep on my healing journey. The guidance and help I have asked for has never failed me and never will, this same assurance that I am not in this alone has been key to my survival and consequently the writing of this book.

It is acknowledged that detoxing is not a course of action you may wish to embark on at this point of your healing journey. However, I strongly recommend that as you read through it you consider implementing some of the activities into your daily routine.

There are hundreds of detoxing programmes available in

books and online which are more structured than the basic detox framework below.

The Inner Child Detox

Every day in every way I am growing stronger and healthier—Louise Hay

Your Inner Child has been subjected to a lot of negative energy over the years not only from when you were young but also as an adult when you were still hurting, and in some cases adopting a self-destructive model, by punishing yourself without often realising the consequences. You may have eating problems or have an addiction to smoking, drinking or drugs. You could be suffering with depression, mental illness or even be self-harming. Or are you a workaholic who drives yourself to destruction to block out the pain of the past.

Your Inner Child is deeply affected by your behaviour. They have been neglected and unable to be free of all the baggage that we made them carry. The best way I believe to get rid of this baggage is to cleanse, just as a caring parent would do for her precious child through love and the desire to give her child the best.

Would a good parent allow a child to remain in soiled nappies all day, give them contaminated food or feed them harmful drugs? Of course not, a caring parent wants only the best for their child. We need to become a good parent to our own Inner Child demonstrating that we care about them. This can be achieved by embarking on the detox programme, which focuses on addressing the physical, psychological, emotional and spiritual needs of your Inner Child.

By making this commitment you are demonstrating to your Inner Child that the adult self is willing to invest love, time and energy, which is a great start to the healing process.

A question for you

When did you last give your body a little bit of tender loving care? We are not talking here about expensive spa treatments, just time out from a busy schedule, maybe a massage, reflexology to name a few, or perhaps an early night, or just getting out in the fresh air and clearing your mind?

Why is it so difficult to set time aside and invest some energy into looking after yourself? Let me tell you whatever the reason it does not get you off the hook as far as your body is concerned.

Have you ever noticed that you are not feeling 100 per cent but are not sick enough to go to bed, that life is an effort and you have lost the zest for life? It could be that your body is telling you that it needs some tender loving care and would benefit from a detox to eradicate toxins and receive good nutrition so that it will give you high performance and reliability.

The Concepts of Cleansing

The phrase "You are what you eat" is a concept that can be observed in all walks of life as more evidence is generated linking health to our western diet. The consequences, of inadequate nutrition leaves our body depleted, with the immune system stretched to its limits as it tries to activate the body's reserves to fight against the toxins that we are daily exposed to through our diet and environmental factors.

What are Toxins?

Toxins come in many different forms they are not new, what is new is the quantity and nature of the toxins we face today. Toxins are harmful substances that pollute and irritate our body putting a strain on the efficiency of our vital organs. When the system becomes over-burdened and unable to cope, toxins build up in the body, this has a negative effect on health and general well-being, which could result in cancer, heart disease and many other health problems.

How Toxic Are You?

Are you suffering from toxic overload?

If you are unsure how toxic you may be, answer the questions below and add up the number of YES answers. The higher the number, the more toxic and in need of a detox you are likely to be.

Food and drink

On a regular basis, do you eat or drink the following:
- Fizzy soft drinks
- White bread and pasta rather than wholemeal varieties
- Mostly non-organic produce
- Fried foods
- Ready-made meals
- Processed foods (canned or frozen sauces and ketchup)
- Sweets and crisps
- Processed meat—ham, bacon, sausage etc.
- Diet products containing aspartame
- Tap water (or use it for cooking and hot drinks)
- Non-organic fruit and vegetables without first peeling or washing them
- Non-organic leafy vegetables without first removing the outer leaves
- Non-organic root vegetables without first peeling them
- Have more than one takeaway a week
- Add salt, including sea salt, to your cooking and at the table
- Regularly exceed healthy drinking guidelines for alcohol
- Re-use fat and cooking oil
- Add sugar to tea and coffee
- Eat less than 5 portions of fruit and vegetables a day

Environment/lifestyle

- Do you live in a town/city?
- Do you walk or run alongside a busy road?
- Do you regularly swim in a chlorinated pool?
- Do you drive a car?

- Do you work in an air-conditioned office?
- Do you use a mobile phone?
- Do you live near an electricity substation or pylons?
- Do you work at a computer on a daily basis?
- Is your home centrally heated?
- Is your home double-glazed?
- Have you recently bought soft furnishings?
- Do you regularly use household cleaning products?
- Do you smoke?
- Do you live near a busy road or power station?
- Do you experience a lot of stress at work and/or at home?

About you

- Do you have dry skin or hair?
- Do you get skin problems, such as eczema or acne?
- Are you constantly tired?
- Do you find your short-term memory is poor?
- Do you get sinus problems?
- Are you constipated or suffer from diarrhoea?
- Do you get night sweats?
- Do you crave sugary foods?
- Do you crave savoury foods?
- Do you frequently get headaches?
- Do you suffer from water retention?
- Do you experience flatulence or bloating?
- Do you have problems sleeping?
- Do you suffer from depression?
- Do you suffer from constant headaches?

It is acknowledged that the test is designed as a mere awareness exercise and individual levels are subject to the efficiency of the liver to eradicate toxins from the body.

Signs of Toxicity

Aches and pains, allergies, angina, anxiety, backache, bad breath, bleeding gums, blocked sinuses, catarrh, cellulite, constant colds and infections, constipation, coughs, dark circle under eyes, depression, difficulty concentrating, fatigue, flatulence and burping, frequent mood swings, furred tongue, headaches, indigestion, insomnia, itchy or red eyes, joint pain, puffiness or water retention, skin rashes, sore throat, spots, sneezing, strong smelling urine, tiredness allergies and food intolerances.

The more symptoms you identify with, the more toxic you are likely to be.

Lifestyle changes

The starting part of any sustained lifestyle change is to embark upon a detox or cleanse, which will eradicate toxins from the body and promote optimum health. It is the forerunner of a new healthy eating regime, which I trust you will embark upon following this programme.

DETOXING IS NO NEW CONCEPT

Detoxing was not a problem to early man as he would periodically fast. Whilst this is still the practise of several religions, today the majority of people never fast. This denies the body the opportunity to cleanse the body of all the toxins that become trapped in the organs and tissues. Early practices aimed at bringing the body into balance and harmony, these included:

- Blood-letting,
- Purgative measures such as inner cleansing,
- Leech Therapy,
- Chinese Cupping
- Sweating
- Administering herbs.

Modern detox programmes do not involve the uses of leeches and bloodletting, I do not think detoxing would be popular if such methods were used today.

The difference between this detox and the hundreds of detox

programmes available is that we will also focus on healing the Inner Child, as part of the detox, by recognising the needs of your Inner Child and taking positive action to nurture them emotionally.

There is no fixed time limit to complete the detox, in relation to how many days you commit to it. View the detox as being a kick start towards adopting a long-term healthier lifestyle.

The detox programme will give you the tools and the motivation you need to succeed but as the famous quote says, like everything in life, **THE MORE YOU PUT IN THE MORE YOU GET OUT**. If at the end of the day you can say you have given the detox the best you were physically able to give, you have succeeded. This is the place you need to aspire to.

The going may get hard and you may have situations which put you under extra pressure and prevent you from fulfilling your daily goals and tasks, or temptation gets the better of you. BUT THAT'S LIFE we learn from our mistakes. What we need to do is try and ensure we are not put in that situation again. What we **DO NOT DO** is throw in the towel and feel a failure.

An essential part of any detox is your commitment to it and staying positive and in control. Affirmations are excellent at working with your subconscious mind, as we have discussed previously.

As you work through the detox programme you will hopefully appreciate how passionate I am about cleansing, it changed my life in more ways than one. Not only was it instrumental in nurturing my Inner Child. It also enabled me to help others, by encouraging them to cleanse and embark upon a healthier lifestyle. This came about when my daughter developed eczema. It covered almost her entire body, her clothes were sticking to her, as the eczema was weeping and very itchy.

The only thing the dermatologist offered, following a skin patch test was steroids and the suggestion that she learnt to live with it. We expressed our concern regarding the steroids.

It was decided this was not the course of action she wanted to take. She sought alternative therapies, homeopathic remedies and Chinese medicine and whilst there was notable improvement the eczema was still evident especially on her face. Following the suggestion from an herbalist we tried a different approach and embarked upon a strict detoxing regime. Within days the eczema was less angry and within a month the eczema had disappeared completely from some areas of her body.

It made me realise that if we had initially started cleansing the body, and eating a healthier diet, by avoiding sugars, dairy and white flour and drinking more water, the previous therapies could have been more effective. I truly believe the starting point for achieving optimum health has to be through cleansing and ridding the body of stored toxins whilst minimising the impact of stress, which is an unavoidable toxin, a product of living.

What is a Detox?

The principle of any detox program is to simply heal the body through cleansing. Detoxing and cleansing are synonymous—they share the same philosophy and outcome in attaining optimum health.

The body has its own set of natural detoxification processes, which work to eliminate the toxins that are indigested every day. The detox will enhance these natural processes, by reducing the amount of food normally eaten and choosing foods that can cleanse the body. The detox will provide the digestive system with a rest allowing it to concentrate on healing itself by eliminating toxins.

Preparing for a detox

The first thing you need to do is to decide when the detox will commence?

As long as you are fit and healthy there is no reason why you should not detox.

There is no right or wrong time of the year to detox, many people choose to start at the beginning of a month or prior to a significant event such as a wedding, birthday or christening. Holidays are always a time to assess the extra pounds that may have crept on, which motivates you to start cleansing. For others it may be that ill health has forced them to take active measures to improve their health.

So now let's start with considering when NOT to detox.

As mentioned, providing that you are fit and healthy there is no reason why you should not embark upon the detox. However, there are some issues that would prevent from doing a detox:

- If you are pregnant or breast feeding
- Directly following a bout of flu, a severe cold or virus
- If you have recently had food poisoning
- If you are recovering from stress as a result of a life

crisis including pressure at work, it would be far more beneficial to wait until your circumstances improve and you can devote the time and attention to cleanse
- If you are on prescriptive drugs check with your doctor first
- A serious medical condition, such as kidney failure, liver disease or diabetes
- If you are recovering from alcohol or drug addiction you must seek medical advice.

The Healing Crisis

At this point I want to draw your attention to the fact that you may experience some side effects during the detox, as a direct result of the toxins, which are circulating around your body via the blood. They can appear at any time during the detox program but are more commonly experienced at the beginning of a detox.

Symptoms include:

- Headaches especially if you are a caffeine addict.
- Feeling tired and lethargic are classic symptoms of the healing crisis.
- Slight nausea as your liver starts to rid itself of its toxins
- Halitosis (bad breath) along with a furry tongue
- Constipation or diarrhoea as your digestive system is put to the test
- Irritability as your body craves for its sugar fix
- Flu like symptoms, shivering, feeling cold
- Insomnia, this is likely to be caused from your active mind
- Skin rashes

Don't be deterred, this is actually a positive sign that your body is working with you getting rid of the stored toxins. The more severe the crisis the more toxic you are!

The symptoms will pass quickly within 24 to 48 hours.

There are certain guidelines that are promoted in every detox so let us consider them now.

Foods to avoid

The list is just a guide, for the detox, whilst it is important to cut back on the items in the list below, better still cut them out altogether; the decision is yours.

- **Alcohol,** toxic to the liver depletes the body of zinc and magnesium
- **Caffeine,** stimulates the nervous system, can cause sleep problems
- **Dairy products,** mucus forming
- **Meat and fish,** aim to reduce the amount consumed, organic if possible
- **Wheat, Gluten,** can cause digestive problems including bloating.
- **Sugar,** linked to obesity and heart disease
- **Salt**, can cause hypertension and fluid retention
- **Pesticides, preservatives and additives**

Realistic Goals

Whilst the aim should be to cut the identified foods out completely, remember the success of the detox is due to realistic goals so if this is too demanding modify it.

For instance, if there is an occasion such as a celebration where you want to have a glass of wine, have one. What you do not want to do is deny yourself so that you feel miserable and annoyed, as in the scheme of things this negative attitude will not be beneficial to the detox.

So many people have a craving for yeast and sugar, and suffer with digestive problems such as bloating, trapped gas and indigestion. If you are one of those individuals, this is a good time to find out. Cut out bread for at least a week before the detox, if you do not notice a reduction in your symptoms, you can have one slice of wholegrain bread a day for the rest of the detox.

So many people are battling with a sugar addiction, a major cause is due to the obsession we previously had with a low-fat food, which contained high percentage of sugar. If you consume excessive amounts of coffee, try and restrict it to one cup a day.

By taking lots of chemical stimulants such as coffee, tea, sugar, alcohol and sugary carbonated drinks we get a boost of energy. The adrenal glands are activated which gives us a high and this can result in anxiety, high blood pressure and insomnia. This prepares the body for engaging in physical or mental activity. When we don't release this stored energy, it produces a crash of energy resulting in a low; we then take more stimulants to create a high and so the circle continues.

List of Cleansing and Health Promoting Activities

- Drinking hot water and lemon everyday
- Consuming one and half to two litres of water daily
- Consuming five or more portions of fruit and vegetables a day
- Eating more raw foods
- Juicing or taking green super foods
- Taking an Epsom salt bath at least once a week
- Castor oil pack once a week
- Daily skin brushing
- Thirty minutes of exercise including daily stretching
- Practising deep breathing exercises.
- Spending some time outdoors each day
- Practising daily meditations and affirmations.

Keeping a Journal

As part of your detox, I would also like you to consider keeping a detox journal, a small notebook is ideal. I have lots of journals, which I have compiled over the years. Many of my childhood memories I shared with you were initially written in journals. The journal will enable you to chart your progress and help keep you motivated whilst providing a source of information for you to reflect on in the future. Carry it with you throughout the day so you can easily record your thoughts. My experience is that whilst working with the Inner Child activities it enabled me to discover some profound facts about myself regarding my behaviour in certain situations. The act of writing it down was therapy in itself.

Planning the Detox

I suggest that you map out your essential commitments such as care of the children and their social activities, Consider, housework, shopping, and any social activities you are involved with. Now write down the all the activities that need to be carried out in relation to time. What time do you normally get up in the morning and what is your regular bedtime? You will now be able to work out how much time you will have each day of the week to construct a realistic detox programme that allows you to select the detox activities in relation to both time and preference. It is important that you have enough time early morning when you can mentally prepare for the day ahead and connect to your Inner Child.

You may need to restructure a little and try and get the rest of the family to support you, the same principle applies if you are working, remember everyone is entitled to a lunch time including you. I am amazed at the amount of people who never take a break, eating lunch at their desks, answering the phone or driving to appointments and eating in the car. Your body deserves better. Even taking time out during the day to recharge will have immense benefits to your overall wellbeing.

I cannot stress enough that you make an honest assessment of what is possible and what you hope to achieve, set realistic goals.

Below is a list of detoxing activities, select the ones that appeal to you. There may be several that you already practice, in that case select others that are a bit more challenging.

Detox Activity List

The aim of the listed activities is to provide you with extra tools to promote your Inner Child detox. They are not compulsory. Be realistic in your choice, consider time, energy and commitment that each individual activity involves before making your decision. This will ensure that you enjoy the detox experience and not experience the disappointment of not achieving your goal.

Select a minimum of two each week.

Please note that the advanced detox activities are for those who have detoxed previously.

- Aim to drink 2 litres of water a day (8 glasses). Discipline yourself to drink one litre by lunch time, and the second litre before retiring; it will flush out toxins, re-hydrate you and give you more energy
- Reduce caffeine. By drastically reducing caffeine intake you will observe skin tone change, experience better quality sleep and a more relaxed approach to life, ideally cut it out all together; try herbal teas instead.
- Herbal teas—try different herbal teas each week until you find one that you like. You can obtain benefits from infusions such as dandelion, which is an excellent diuretic, which aids fluid retention. You can also add dandelion leaves to salads.
- Cut out all red meats for a month along with the "3 Ss"—Sugar, Salt and Stimulants. Give your digestive system a rest.
- Carry out a mini fast. Eat your last meal before 6.00pm and then leave breakfast until after 9.00am the following day. Try to make the meals either side of your mini fast based on organic fruit and vegetables.
- Do 30 minutes of exercise every other day or 15 minutes every day. Walk to work, climb stairs, go to an aerobics class, even housework is a form of exercise
- Dry skin brushing, using a soft brush, in a sweeping stroke, gently brush upwards from feet to knees, knees to hips, both legs front and back, from hands up the arms to the shoulders and the torso, brush towards the

heart and cover the whole body.

- Epsom salt bath. Have a hot bath with two cups of Epsom salts. Stay in the bath for at least 30 minutes and massage the skin. Wrap up warmly or go to bed, feel the toxins purge from your body. Add a few drops of essential oils to make it an even nicer experience.

- Learn to enjoy your food by chewing at least 20 times. This will aid digestion by activating digestive enzymes to break down your food. Don't eat on the move.

- Speed up the detox by having a reflexology treatment to stimulate all eliminatory organs to release the stored toxins.

- Detox your tongue. Scrape your tongue with your toothbrush and remove all the bacteria that lives there, this will reduce any infections in the mouth and gums.

- Apply a castor oil pack to the abdomen and liver area. Cover with cling film and place a hot water bottle or heat pack to the area. This will help to soften impacted faeces that can lodge in the pockets of the colon.

- If you suffer from bloating, cut out all yeast, wheat and sugar for a week and monitor the effects.

- Give your immune system a boost by taking a garlic capsule daily, garlic is also anti-bacterial and anti-fungal and is reputed to slow down the ageing process.

- Treat yourself to a massage using aromatherapy oils. Try rosemary to balance your moods or have a long soak in a warm bath using lemongrass or lavender.

- Reduce stress. Do something that will make you laugh; watch a funny film, read a funny book. Go on have a good giggle

- Try to eat organic food for a week and notice the difference in both taste and texture.

- Take note of your posture, try and make a conscious effort to sit up straight and avoid slumping this will help your digestive organs to work more efficiently during the detox.

- Practise deep therapeutic breathing in the fresh air. Breathe in through your nose to a count of 4, take the air to the abdomen hold for a count of 4, Breathe out through your mouth for 8 seconds.

- Yoga or Pilates can relax tone and invigorate. Establish a daily routine of stretches to increase flexibility.

- Give your face a detox by brushing it with a soft toothbrush in an upwards direction. This will stimulate circulation remove dead cells and tone up facial muscles.
- Invest time and energy into carrying out regular detox programmes to ensure that you promote optimum health and wellbeing.
- Have a day when you make a conscious effort not to cross your legs; it is bad for circulation as it puts extra pressure on your heart.
- Research Colon Hydrotherapy, book a treatment if it appeals to you it will help to cleanse the bowel and help eliminate toxins.
- Help your detox by massaging aromatherapy oils into your feet. Fennel, juniper or geranium are all good for detoxing
- To relieve tension, have a good scream!! Seriously it will release inner tension and leave you feeling calmer and more peaceful. Notice how at sports gatherings especially football how people shout and bawl. Excellent stress relief
- Do some facial exercises, look in a mirror and open your mouth as wide as you can or stick out your tongue move your jaw up and down and feel all the tension you hold in your jaw relax away

ADVANCED

- Try a 24 hour water fast, following your last meal (before 7.00pm) eat nothing until the following day at 7.00pm. Ensure that you drink at least 2 litres of water during the fast.
- Every day take one tablespoon of apple cider vinegar with a teaspoonful of honey. The malic acid in the vinegar is both cleansing and has an alkaline effect on the body
- Do a simple liver cleanse for a period of seven days, which will speed up the detoxification process. Place 6 tablespoons of lemon juice, 3 tablespoons of virgin olive oil, 1 small crushed, garlic clove, pinch of grated ginger whisk in a blender and drink immediately, do not eat for at least an hour after.

- Research the benefits of oil pulling. Prior to eating in the morning place ½ or a tablespoon of organic virgin coconut oil into your mouth or castor oil, slowly swish the oil around making sure the oil reaches every area of your mouth. Swish for ten minutes and do not swallow the oil. Spit out the oil and rise with water. Clean your teeth afterwards. Oil pulling is a powerful way of detoxing the body it removes toxins bacteria and parasites from the mouth it will reduce plaque, whiten your teeth and freshen your breath.
- Give yourself an enema. It is not as daunting as it sounds. The kits are available online. They can help maintain a healthy bowel especially if constipation is a problem
- Administer a coffee enema. The coffee stimulates the liver to produce an anti-cancer enzyme. It also boosts your energy levels. Avoid having one in the evening, the caffeine may put you on a high alert, not what you desire when trying to sleep.
- Have one day when you eat nothing but raw foods. This gives you optimum nutrition. Do some research into the benefits of raw foods.

Inner Child Activity List

The list consists of varied activities designed to help you maintain a relationship with your Inner Child. Aim to include at least two into your daily routine. You may have already done the basic Inner Child workout in Part Three. The activities are tools for helping to maintain that relationship.

- Every morning look into the mirror and talk to your Inner Child. Start by reminding them that you love them. Tell them it is going to be a good day and they have no need to be afraid, they are safe now and you are aware of all their needs.
- Choose an affirmation relating to your Inner Child and aim to say it at least 20 times a day to reinforce your commitment to them.

- Throughout the day take out the picture of you when you were a child and kiss it lovingly. Or simply just look at the picture and tell your Inner Child that you love them. Placing the photograph near your heart is a lovely way of maintaining the bond you have with your Inner Child.
- Recall an activity you did as a child, which you enjoyed. It could involve playing board games, doing a jigsaw, reading a book you read in your childhood, roller skating, ball games, swimming, baking special cakes you associate with your childhood. It is recognised that there may be some activities that invoke painful memories. If this is the case, just acknowledge them knowing that when you are stronger emotionally you will want to become involved in the activity as a method of testing yourself in relation to how far you have come in your recovery.
- Spend time with children or simply observe them, listen to the excitement in their voices, how happy they appear. Listen to a child laughing; it's infectious. For many victims of child abuse laughter is not an automatic response. They have learnt to shut down their emotions making them unable to express their emotions especially in relation to laughing and crying.
- If you are one of those individuals, ask yourself when did you last laugh? I mean really laugh until it hurts, till the tears are running down your face and you cannot stop.
- No one wants to cry. We are socialised into believing that crying is a sign of weakness especially in boys. As a little child it is acceptable to cry, in fact crying is the natural emotion for being heard and having our needs met. We grow up seeing crying as a childhood activity that we have grown out of. Crying is therapeutic and if not released can manifest in several physical

conditions according to Louise Hay as we discussed in Part Three.

- If you cannot cry, who avoids watching sad movies or cannot cry even at the loss of someone close it is an area you need to address. You have shut down emotionally. During the detox period try and watch a sad movie in an attempt to open up to your emotional self and reach out to that hurting Inner Child.
- During each day make a conscious effort to tell your Inner Child that they are doing well and let them hear praise from you as praise and encouragement are something that your Inner Child has been deprived of. Think how good it makes you feel when someone gives you praise for something you have achieved or simply for the way you look. Let your Inner Child hear them words absorb them deep within. If it helps when saying them place your hand over your heart to make the words even more special.
- Treat yourself, all children love to be treated it makes them feel special. As a child you may have felt that treats didn't flow your way, so now it's the time to indulge—remember you now deserve only the best. It doesn't have to be an expensive treat, it can be simply going out for the evening, going to the cinema, having your hair or nails done, going for a massage. Something that makes you feel good about yourself. During the four weeks plan a special treat each week. At the end of the detox have a very special treat organised. Enjoy planning for this special event.

Basic Inner Child Detox Schedule. (BIDS)

The basic Inner Child detox schedule (BIDS) is a summary of the main activities which you could include in your detox plan.

- Each morning wake-up thirty minutes early to allow time for the extra detox activities
- Before getting out of bed fill your head with positive thoughts for the day
- Carry out some stretching exercises
- Body brushing prior to your shower
- Connect to your Inner Child
- Hot water and lemon in the morning
- Take a probiotic daily
- Use positive affirmations throughout the day
- Aim to drink two litres of water each day
- Eat three healthy meals a day
- Snack only on healthy options
- Practise mindful breathing
- Carry out at least one detox activity you selected from the detox list
- Carry out at least two Inner Child activities you selected from the list.
- Engage in some form of exercise
- Carry out Donna Eden's energy activities
- Be conscious of any negative thoughts
- Spend some time relaxing
- Be selective with what you watch on television
- Aim to have at least two early nights each week
- Have at least one Epsom salt bath during the week
- Have one castor oil pack, within the week.
- Write in your journal everyday
-

Detox your mind

A positive mind is required for the detox programme, in fact mental fitness is just as important as physical fitness. You need to focus on the positive and avoid dwelling on negative thoughts, which activate a downward spiral producing low self-esteem and depressive thoughts. There are active steps you can implement, which will change the way you think and consequently produce more happiness and fulfilment. As previously discussed, in recent years there has been an awareness of the power of the subconscious mind along with the concept of the Law of Attraction, this is an amazing concept and if you are interested there is a wealth of information out there. Rhonda Byrne's *The Secret* is a good place to start, as discussed previously.

We can attract anything we want by changing our thinking away from the negative to the positive. This week try and integrate positive thoughts whilst becoming aware of any negative thoughts that occur. Enter these unwanted thoughts in your journal, followed by how you were able to turn a negative thought into a positive. Use the elastic band activity described previously to quickly discharge negative thoughts.

Smile at three people, ideally people you have no contact with. Smiling is infectious, it may feel uncomfortable at first especially if the person doesn't respond but I guarantee the majority of people will smile back at you. Smiling has borrowed benefits in that you cannot smile and look miserable at the same time. It will lift your spirit, it is positive energy, the more you work with positive energy and higher frequencies the more benefits you will experience just by focusing on the positive and replacing any negative thoughts with positive ones.

Habits of Happy People

Due to the implications of living with the shame of child sexual abuse, we can remain numb to our emotions and deny the gift of happiness. The aim of the book was to provide you with the tools and a framework for your personal journey of recovery. With any project or challenge a successful outcome should promote a sense of achievement and fulfilment along with a degree of happiness. For many happiness has been denied as a consequence of the coping strategies adopted in childhood, and the concept of happiness is nothing more than an illusion.

Five Important Questions

Are you happy? How do you define happiness? What makes you happy? Do you deny yourself the right to experience happiness? Is it easier to relate to the emotions associated with being unhappy than being happy?

Happiness is something that I feel evaded me for many years through being numb to any emotions including the gift of happiness.

As we know our childhood may have been responsible for many habits we exhibit, but these learnt habits can also be the cause of our despondency and apathy to life. Too many people wait for the circumstances of their lives to change before they believe they can ever be happy. They attribute the pursuit of being happy to a time when they have more money, or they have lost weight, finding the right partner or having a better job. The problem is waiting for something or someone to make you happy is not the remedy to be happy. Happiness comes from within, not through wealth, having the perfect body, or perfect looks. It cannot be sought through relationships. To be happy is your birth right. Your Inner Child has not only been denied love and attention, rarely had the opportunity to experience happiness. When you accept that true happiness comes from within and can be learnt by implementing positive actions or positive habits into your life, happiness will naturally evolve.

By the end of the Inner Child detox, I want you to experience true happiness. It is a skill and is accessible by simply engaging in a certain set of new habits.

People who are happy the majority of the time have created an inner peace in their lives through positive habits that enhance their life bringing a depth of happiness that is not reliant on other people or circumstances.

All the activities you have engaged in during the detox have been positive lifestyle changes, which are linked to improved health and wellbeing and also happiness. Have you observed that often the behaviour patterns or habits of happy people are in fact the same habits as those who lead a healthy lifestyle?

In the Inner Child detox, we covered some of the essential components of detoxing and cleansing in the pursuit of reclaiming optimum health and wellbeing. They included eating nutritional foods, what you eat can impact on your mood and energy levels. Exercise, which boosts the level of brain chemicals such as serotonin, dopamine and norepinephrine, which may help with stress and depression. Meditation helps to keep your mind focused, calms inner nerves and supports inner peace. Adopt the philosophy of the half full glass and not the half empty glass scenario. De-clutter both your mind and home. The positive impact they collectively produce will establish a structured framework for the pursuit of happiness but only if you can relate to it.

Let's now consider some of the other habits that you can adopt in the pursuit of happiness.

There are several recognised habits or behaviour patterns below that are especially relevant to healing the Inner Child.

Let go of grudges—One thing that will keep you anchored to the past is your unwillingness to forgive if you are holding on to anger, resentment, hurt and a host of other negative emotions that we have discussed previously.

Don't compare yourself to others—Never compare yourself to those around you, don't measure or compare or compete with others. You are unique and special in your own right. Allow your Inner Child, your true self to grow and flourish. Pursue your own goals not the goals set out by others. Use the affirmations throughout the book until you believe in your own self-worth.

You do not need the approval of others—This is an important habit to break. Often to gain the love and attention of others especially our parents and other important care providers we become people pleasers. This is reflected in our habits and behaviour, to the detriment of not being able to follow our own heart's desires for the need of gaining approval of others.

Spend time with positive people—As we have discovered through the Law of Attraction, like attracts like. You will already be aware that certain friends make you feel good, their energy is contagious making you feel good just by being around them. You will have other friends or even family members who are negative in their outlook; everything is an issue or crisis. This negativity is also contagious—it drains you and can affect your mood.

Establish personal control—Stop letting other people control your life by dictating the way you live. Break the mould and pursue your own goals and dreams. Don't deny your Inner Child the freedom to discover their self-worth.

Be kind and considerate to others—The world would be a better place if everyone treated others as they would like to be treated. Through being kind to others your brain releases feel-good hormones like serotonin. You can extend this by doing one good deed for someone every day, it doesn't have to be anything of great magnitude, the simple act of being a considerate driver, giving way to other traffic, making a small donation to charity, buying a hot drink for a friend, ringing or visiting an elderly relative, or sending a card to someone who is going through a traumatic time in their lives. The list is endless, but the results are the same. It also interconnects to the Law of Attraction, in that what you give you will receive back. Try it and see.

Problems are just Challenges—When you are confronted with a problem change your mindset and view it as a challenge and an opportunity to learn and grow. Better still completely remove the word "problem" from your vocabulary.

Let Gratitude become a way of life—A major component of happiness is to constantly express gratitude throughout the day. It is reported that Albert Einstein would say "Thank you" at least one hundred times a day. Ho'oponopono (the Hawaiian Healing Therapy) embraces gratitude in its teachings. The concept of gratitude has been linked to decreased stress, happier moods, having a positive outlook and better physical health. You can always discover things to be grateful especially when you consider the plight of those living in extreme poverty or being subjected to health related, problems.

Avoid stressing about the small stuff—Happy people have a filter, which ensures that they are not affected by life's little irritations. If the issue will not be relevant in a month, a year or even tomorrow, they put it into context and don't stress about it. Imagine how much energy is wasted in things that really don't matter in the scheme of things. Does it really matter if the supermarket doesn't have green bananas, or the queue for petrol is too long, will it really cause major implications?

Material things don't make you happy—There is considerable research that demonstrates that money and material possessions don't bring sustained happiness. Once you have acquired the item and realised it gave you only a minimal amount of satisfaction, you then focus on your next project in the belief that it will make you happy and bring you contentment. The truth is being truly happy comes from within and cannot be purchased.

Stop seeing yourself as a victim—Whilst it is acknowledged that you were the innocent victim in the past, it doesn't equate that you continue to see yourself as the victim in every situation by fostering the belief that "life is out to get me and there is nothing I can do about it". This belief is just an attitude you may have unwillingly adopted by previous life events. It can become a self-fulfilling philosophy and will keep you enslaved to the past. Happy people refuse to see themselves as being life's victims.

Stop blaming others for your past—We live in a "blame society" it is almost like a natural reaction to blame someone else. When you do something wrong it's always someone else's fault, instead of taking responsibility for our own actions and being accountable. The word "sorry" is not used often enough. We all make mistakes, but happy people take responsibility for their own mistakes and learn from them. However, if as a child you were blamed for everything and made a scapegoat you will have experienced the hurt and frustration of being blamed for other people's mistakes. Into adulthood it may have left its scar because you constantly feel the need to use the word "sorry" for your actions often when it is not needed. It is a question of getting the balance right.

Dream big—Your childhood may have denied you so much, your dreams and ambitions, whilst never being allowed to flourish, you were prevented from discovering your true self and being aware of your true potential. Now is the time to **Dream Big**, you have the power within yourself to accomplish great things **You Deserve It.**

A structured routine—The Inner Child detox schedule establishes a routine, which not only helped you to be more organised, which in turn minimises the effects of everyday stress that we are all subjected to. By waking up at the same time each morning you establish your circadian rhythm and feel more energised throughout the day. It is the habit of many successful individuals who find that it accelerates productivity and focus. The act of waking up early in the morning has been instrumental in writing this book. The majority of the book has been written before commencing my working routine.

Happy people choose to be happy—By making a conscious effort to review your habits, in the pursuit of happiness, is an amazing thing to embark, upon it will bring change and results in ways you could never envisage. As you take control of your happiness you will make those around you happier too, Remember, happiness is contagious.

Some of the benefits you may experience at the end of your Detox.

There will be marked differences within your body and energy levels.
You will feel more confident as you have successfully achieved your aim through setting realistic achievable goals.
You will have established a closer relationship with your Inner Child, which will continue to develop as you make a conscious effort each day to communicate with your Inner Child.
The mention of child sexual abuse will no longer have the same impact on you physically and mentally.
Your skin, hair and nails will have benefited by both the cleansing and the nurturing.
If after the detox you have not seen any marked health

improvements, I would investigate the role of vitamins and supplements, or better still see a nutritionist or visit an independent health shop.

Due to the regular exercises that you carried out during the detox program your posture will have improved. If you have observed any intense pain or have limited flexibility due to discomfort it may be beneficial to get to visit a chiropractor or have it checked out by a GP.

If you struggled with digestive problems, they should have improved due to your improved diet and your response to the stresses of life, by being more organised and adopting stress-reducing activities. If you are still suffering with digestive problems or intense bloating, seek the advice of a health professional.

Following the end of your planned detox It is up to you how you start to introduce some of the things that you have been avoiding during the Detox. I know that for many people it is quite a disappointment when they introduce bread, chocolate, sugar or alcohol back into their diet, they have an immediate negative reaction to the foods they have been avoiding. This makes them re-assess their previous diet and carry on avoiding the foods that their body is intolerant or sensitive to. On the emotional front I hope you see yourself no longer a slave to the past, and that you truly believe that you are worthy of loving yourself.

The Final Chapter—Actions Speak Louder Than Words

The final chapter is written by you.

Now having read the book, you are presented with further choices. Before you even commenced reading the book you had a choice as to how you were going to read it. According to publishers there are three different ways that individuals read a book according to their own individual reading style:

1. Read the first and last chapter and bits in between but never read an entire book start to end.
2. Diligently work through an entire book setting time aside to work through the activities.
3. Read the entire book in a few hours by skipping the suggested activities.

Whichever method appeals to you is not important, it's the message of the book that is of value and how it resonates with you.

The next choice you now have to make is what you do with the information the book contained:

1. Do nothing and stay trapped remaining a silent victim.
2. Make a conscious decision now to step out on to the road of recovery and discover your true self, by embarking on your healing journey
3. Acknowledge the need to start your healing journey but need more support

At this point I need to reinforce what I said in the introduction regarding working with a qualified counsellor who is trained in working with victims of child sexual abuse. Through reading the book you may now have recognised that you do need more intense therapy and the support of a therapist to assist you in your recovery. I also acknowledge that there will be those who are not ready to fully commit to the full program. I suggest that you try just one of the activities in the program as the first step to coming out and starting your healing journey. My hope is that the message of the book will have challenged you to initiate change. The book is of no value if like an instruction manual that comes with an appliance, the advice it contains is ignored once it has been read. I hope that *I Am NOT A Dirty Bitch* has been more than an instruction manual. It has been a journey of discovery and a catalyst to initiate change in your life.

In the introduction I used the words 'Kindred Spirit', hopefully by identifying with my journey you will have been empowered to acknowledge your power and take control of your future through the knowledge that you are not alone. Whilst the path you choose will follow a different route from mine, we all share a common bond. We are united through our past and we can remain united in the present and the future as you take the first step on your journey of recovery. The first step is always the hardest one to take, simply by acknowledging that your childhood is still having a detrimental effect especially if it involved sexual abuse, is a good starting point.

As I discovered you have no idea how many others you can empower simply by coming out and being identified as a victim of child sexual abuse. It only takes that first step. If you used the book as a tool to instigate even the slightest change it will have achieved its aim but only you can write the conclusion.

I believe that by breaking the shame-game collectively, we can make a difference to others and consequently society at large. We have a responsibility to our children and our children's children to stand united as one collective voice. The louder we shout the more we will be heard. Through our collective voices, I truly believe we can make a difference and stop innocent children having to endure the pain and emotional trauma we were subjected to. We need more people like Andy Woodward, who through his personal experience of child sexual abuse, came out of the shame-game and brought sexual abuse that existed in football to the media's attention.

Remember child sexual abuse is allowed to flourish by keeping it a dark secret. The more people who come out of hiding and are willing to be identified as victims, the more we can promote awareness of the epidemic of child sexual abuse that is still impacting on the lives of so many individuals. Child sexual abuse must be eradicated. No child should have to live with the consequences of such a violation, which acts like a festering wound that never heals as we have discovered.

I can offer no magic words that will help to convince that you deserve to be loved and to experience true happiness, which radiates from within. The day you can look into a mirror and say "I love you" will be the day your past has no longer any power over you. My final words are:

The greatest healing tool is love and the greatest abuse is to not love yourself.

In an attempt to continue to help and support individuals, whose childhood is still dictating the future. I have become a Life coach and devised a program known as LIGAT Let it go and thrive. The program allows individuals to discover their inner self limiting beliefs
and then work towards their personal goals.

There are six pillars, which is woven into the LIGAT program:

1. Stillness and connect to a Higher Source
2. Letting go of past trauma
3. Practising daily acts of gratitude
4. Discovering your creativity
5. Forgiveness of self and others

6. Promoting self love and happiness

If you want to learn more go to Lynnemcdougall.com.

Afterword

My childhood presented many challenges that I have shared with you. In retrospect I now questioned how I manage to survive with so little help and support. So many incidents could have been responsible for me taking a different course as I have seen happen to others especially whilst working with the homeless. The truth is I do know; it is summed up in the saying "There but for the grace of God go I". I believe that there is a "Higher Power" or a "Man Upstairs". Many times, in the depth of pain tiny miracles have occurred that cannot be explained. I deliberated long and hard if I should include any reference to the spiritual realm, which played such an important role both in my recovery and enabling me to survive my childhood eventually being able to see it in a positive way, by making me the person I am today.

By not acknowledging a Higher Power I feel that I would not be giving you the full story, or an honest account of my journey.

I have selected incidents demonstrating that despite living in a home without love and affection and being so unhappy there was always someone or something helping me; I was never truly alone.

Please read the following with an open mind. The help and strength I received does not belong to any particular religious sect, it is a connection to a Higher Power, which is available to everyone.

As I have relived the memories of my childhood, some of the incidents have been more painful than others. One such incident that evoked emotional trauma was when I was told by my father, that I was not his biological daughter. I felt that I had lost my identity; I was no longer who I believed I was. I am sure it would have been less traumatic if I heard that my father had died.

As a child I had carried a torch for my father always defending him, as I believed that he was innocent and that he did love me. I had come to terms with the fact that he made no attempt to see me, when my mother left him. Believing that he was too busy working to look after me. In retrospect I think I was in denial but at the time it was my coping strategy to deal with rejection.

Whilst I did share the incident with you, I did not disclose how the incident became a crucial learning experience. I had called to see my father after visiting my grandma who lived in the same town. My two young daughters with me at the time and were playing in the lounge. His wife was preparing lunch in the kitchen. My father went into the kitchen and then asked me to come through. I entered the kitchen, and they closed the door. I remember clearly his wife saying, "Your father has something to tell you". He then announced as if he was reciting from a book. "I have loved you as my own daughter, but I am not your father."

I remained silent as he calmly explained that he had been injured during the war and was impotent and so could not be my biological father or that of my siblings. It had such an impact on me that I remember it was 11.40am according to their kitchen clock. I was offered lunch but declined the offer, saying I needed to get back home. He attempted to explain how much he had loved me despite me not being his child. In that moment I realised that he had never loved me. He too had intensely hurt me as I once again experienced the pain of rejection. It made me feel worthless. Even if it were, true what purpose would it serve to tell me now, after all these years?

At 11.35am that day I thought I knew who I was, and at 11.40am the person I thought I was no longer existed. I felt like a lifeline had been severed. The realisation that my father had never loved me hit me hard. It destroyed the childhood trust I had always carried for him.

I was annoyed with myself for not seeing the truth earlier. Many questions flooded my mind. Who am I? Why couldn't I have had parents who loved and supported me?

Who had ever been there for me? Certainly not my mother or father. When I had no questions left. I heard an audible voice, "I am your Heavenly Father I have always been here, you are my child, I love you". Along with words came a feeling of inner strength, as the truth of the words resonated with me. I had heard that voice and experienced that inner strength, that inner knowing several times before. I was never alone even in the darkest times including that day.

This connection to something beyond myself has been intertwined throughout my life, the way that the right people came into my life at the right time. Consider the time when my mother and my siblings had been to social services when she had left my stepfather. How my friend's mother from church was passing by and offered to accommodate us.

My first job involved working for a wonderful caring lady in her chemist shop, she nurtured and cared for me, often giving me gifts and bringing me lunch. There were other human angels that appeared to support and encourage me. A guide leader encouraged me, by bringing me the ingredients, so that I could pass my guide badges for homemaking and cookery.

Apart from the kind caring individuals there were several occasions when a spiritual dimension was evident protecting and caring for me.

I remember the experience of not truly being alone happened several times when I was living with my mother and stepfather. As you may recall life was very structured when we were living with my stepfather. I had always to be home by 9pm. One particular Saturday night I had gone to church and the concert finished late. I would normally have slipped away before it had finished, but on this occasion, I forgot the time. I was horrified to discover it was already 9pm. Walking home I feared what was to come from my mother and stepfather for being late. I prayed with all my heart that I wouldn't be punished. I walked into the house over thirty minutes late and apologised. To be met with the words from my mother "You had better go straight to bed", my stepfather said nothing. I was amazed, any other times I would have punished for being disobedient, but tonight I was just told to go to bed. I know that it seems quite insignificant, but it was such a major event that made me believe in the power of prayer, which have been a major coping strategy for me throughout the years.

Another profound incident happened several years ago, we were broken into during the night whilst we were asleep. Many valuable things were taken along with my laptop. Incredibly the intruders removed the USB stick and left it on the desk. It contained many of the childhood stories that have been shared in the book. I believe this was another act of spiritual intervention. If the USB stick had been taken many of the stories could not have been accurately duplicated, which questions if this book would have ever been written.

The Final Letting Go

Since the launch of my book so many people have shared with me how as a child they too were sexually abused. What is even more revealing is that for several of them I was the first person they had shared their secret with.

Another revelation that came to light is the high correlation between child sexual abuse and a poor relationship with their mothers, especially in the formative years.

Regarding my own mother I allowed her to come back into my life in 2017, this was several weeks after my book had been printed. Whilst I have no regrets about her becoming involved in my life again, it was a challenging time as she continued to emotionally abuse me as I tried once again to try and gain her love.

It was one of those occasions that wasn't planned it just evolved. I had taken Christmas presents to my sister-in-law, who asked me to drop off Christmas gifts for my mother on our way home as we would drive near to where my mother lived. My brother had died in July that year and my sister-in-law didn't drive. The outcome was that I became emotionally involved with my mother again and the mind games recommenced.

Initially every time I had contact with my mother, she made me feel dirty to the point that I felt the need to have a shower, it also made me feel anxious as I became her main care provider by ensuring her needs became a priority.

She remained in my life from December 2017 to the 30th December, 2018 when she passed away, in a nursing home near to where I live. Prior to moving her nearer to me I visited her at least once a week and spoke to her daily on the phone.

I became power of attorney, which allowed me to sort out her debts and do her weekly shopping, this included purchasing a wheelchair and a new reclining chair along with buying her new clothes.

Despite the distance, which could often take up to four hours round trip I used to take her out weekly to garden centers or for lunch. I was able to arrange a birthday party for her at a restaurant for the family to celebrate her ninetieth birthday. However, it was never enough to stop her from her using cruel words. against me, it appeared whatever I did for her never merited any gratitude.

I had gone to visit her one Sunday, it was Remembrance Day, she was asleep in the main lounge. I gently stroked her hand and said, "hello mum", she refused to open her eyes and acknowledge me. A member of staff who had observed the scene called me over to her. She asked me why I allowed my mother to ignore me. Apparently, my mother had been interacting with other residents and staff until she saw me approaching then pretended to be asleep.

A few weeks before she passed, I was with her in her room when a care assistant entered, my mother looked directly at me and said, "I love her" The care assistant laughed and replied, "Sheila, you only love me because you love my scones". Later my husband entered the room again she said looking directly at me 'I love him, he is the best son-in-law in the world".

When it was time to leave, I kissed her on her forehead, and she responded by saying in a stern voice" I love you really". There are no words to adequately describe how that made me feel. I went through the whole grieving process again as I admitted to myself that nothing had changed, my mother was never going to be able to tell me she really loved me or appreciate anything I did for her.

My final act of letting go was when I visited her alone in the chapel of rest. I told her that despite never being able to truly love me I had done everything in my power to make her love me. In that moment I felt a tremendous surge of love towards her and with it came the knowing that she was the hurting frightened child not me. Through her neglect I had become me.

Acknowledgements

Wayne, Diane and Shaun, my siblings who shared the trauma of my childhood; sadly, my two brothers are now deceased.

My husband, Ian, who, despite not being able to share my emotional journey, has given me the time and space to discover the truth

Libby Mangham who took on the task of proof reading, the early draft copies.

Ian Briscoe who is more than a good neighbour; he not only carried out a structural edit, without his guidance and patience the book would have never been published.

Zoe Hannan and Steven Pearson, an answer to prayer for editing and type setting the revised edition.

My close friend Karen Helmn who offered practical assistance with printing the many drafts.

Gillian Edwards for her expert guidance and practical help regarding publishers and book cover agents

Tony Clarkson for writing the foreword and for his encouragement and words of wisdom.

Wendy Webster from Graphix Direct for the brilliant book cover design.

David Harrison who offered guidance and support.

Nigel Peace at Local Legend who took an interest in the manuscript and wrote a review.

My mother who has been my greatest teacher.

Poppet who sacrificed the majority of her childhood.

To my spiritual companions, who have loved supported and sustained me and continue to do so.

Bibliography

Part One

DAVIS, L. 1999: *The Courage to Heal Workbook: A Guide for Women and Men Survivors of Child Sexual Abuse.* Harper Perennial, New York.

Hall, L. & Lloyd, S. 1993: *Surviving Child Sexual Abuse: A Handbook For Helping Women Challenge Their Past.* Routledge, Oxford, UK.

Preston, S. 2013: *Sarah's Story – They cruelly stole my childhood. Here is my story of recovery and triumph.* John Blake.

Help lines and Support Agencies:
NSPCC Helpline 0800 800 5000
help@nspcc.org.uk

Childline 0800 1111
www.childline.org.uk

The Survivors Trust. National Helpline; support advice and information
0800 801 0818
www.napac.org.uk

The National Association of People Abused in Childhood (NAPAC)
0808 801 0331
www.napac.org.uk

The Lantern Project. Supporting Victims of Childhood Sexual Abuse
0151 606 4810
email: lanternproject@yahoo.com

Adult Survivor Support Services Lancashire www. csasupportlancashire.com

References:
Felitti, Vincent J. 2002: *Adverse Childhood experiences study 1995-1997. Landmark in Epidemiological Research*

Longfield, A., Children Commissioner for England: *The Truth about Child Sex Abuse.* BBC 2, Documentary. 24th November 2015

Part Two
Levin, A. 27th February 2017: *My Mother Was A Cruel And Horrid Women:* Daily Mail

Dr. McBride, K. 2008: *Will I Ever Be Good Enough? Healing `the Daughters Of Narcissistic Mothers*

Morrigan D. 2013: *You're Not Crazy – It's Your Mother: Understanding and healing for daughters of narcissistic mothers.* Darton, Longham & Todd Ltd, London

Pen, M. 2014: *Good Mother Bad Daughter? - An Adult Daughter's Guide To Coping With An Emotionally Abusive Mother.* Self-Published

Part Three
Bradshaw, J. 2014: *Homecoming: Reclaiming and Championing Your Inner Child*: CPI group UK

Engel, B. 1991: *The Right to Innocence: Healing the Trauma of Childhood Sexual Abuse: A Therapeutic 7-Step Self Help Program for Men and Women, Including How to Choose a Therapist and Find a Support Group.* The Random House Publishing Group. California

Parks, P. 1990: *Rescuing The Inner Child: Therapy for Adults Sexually Abused as Children.* Sovereign Press Ltd. Victoria Australia

Smalley, G. & Trent, J PHD: *The Blessing. No Matter what*

our age, our parent's approval affects the way we view ourselves. Thomas Nelson, Nashville USA

Taylor, C.L. 1991: *The Inner Child Workbook: What to do with your past when it won't go away.* Penguin Putman, New York

Whitfield, C.L. 1987: *Healing the Child Within: Discovery and Recovery for Adult Children of Dysfunctional Families*: Health Communication Inc., Florida

Whitfield, C. L. 1990: *A Gift to Myself. Personal Workbook and Guide to the Best Selling Healing the Child Within:* Health Communication Inc., Florida

Part Four

Ball, S. 2005: *The Bach Remedy Workbook: A Study course in Bach Flower Remedies.* Random House, UK

Bays, B. 1999: *The Journey An Extraordinary Guide For Healing Your Life And Setting Yourself Free.* Element, Harper-Collins London

Borysenko, J. PhD. 2007: *Minding the Body Mending the Mind.* Perseus Book Group. New York

Byrne, R. 2006: *The Secret.* Beyond Books. Oregon USA

Byrne, R. 2010: *The Power.* Simon Schuster UK Ltd

Cooper, D. 2004: *Angel Inspiration: How to Change Your World with the Angels.* Hodder and Stoughton. London

Eden, D. & Feinstein, D. 2012: *Energy Medicine: Balancing Your Body's Energy for Optimal Health, Joy and Vitality.* Piatkus Books. London

Ellis, R. 2002: *Reiki and the Seven Chakras: Your Essential Guide.* Vermilion- Books, London

Hartmann, S. 2003: *Adventures in EFT: A Practical Guide*

to Emotional Freedom Tapping Techniques. Dragon Rising Publishing, Eastbourne, UK

Hay, L. 1989: *Heal Your Body: The Mental Causes for Physical Illnesses and the Metaphysical Way to Overcome Them.* Hay House UK Ltd

Hay, L. 2005: *You Can Heal your Life.* Hay House UK Ltd

Hess, P. 2008: *Singing Bowls for Health and Inner Harmony Through Sound Massage According to Peter Hess.* Verlag Peter Hess Germany 2008

Garson-Shapiro, J. 1995: *The Flower Remedy Book, A Comprehensive Guide to Over 700 Flower Essences.* North-Atlantic Books, California

Loyd, A. PhD. ND. with Johnson, B. MD. DO. NMD. 2011: *The Healing Code: 6 minutes to Heal the Source of Your Health, Success, or Relationship Issues.* Grand Central Life, & Style New York

Permutt, P. 2007: *The Crystal Healer: Crystal Prescription That Will Change Your Life Forever.* CICO Books. London

McDougall, L. 2008: *Wellsprings Detox Program.* 2008. Personal Guru. Preston Lancashire UK

Dr. Mercola, J. 2013: *22 Positive Habits of Happy People.* On line 8th April 2013

Stein, D. 1995: *Essential Reiki: A Complete Guide to an Ancient Healing Art.* Crossing Press, California

Vitale, J. 2008: *Hawaiian System for Health Wealth and Peace,* John Wiley and Sons. New Jersey

Virtue, PhD. 2005: *Angel Therapy, Healing Messages for Every Area of Your Life.* Hay House Inc. California

Were, K. 2007: *Help Yourself to Happiness.* 2007. Geddes & Grosset. Glasgow.